The Pocket Mortgage Guide

The Pocket Mortgage Guide

60 of the Most Important Questions and Answers About Your Home Loan

Jack Guttentag
"The Mortgage Professor"

McGraw-Hill
New York Chicago San Francisco Lisbon
London Madrid Mexico City Milan New Delhi
San Juan Seoul Singapore Sydney Toronto

The McGraw-Hill Companies

1 2 3 4 5 6 7 8 9 0 AGM/AGM 0 9 8 7 6 5 4 3

ISBN 0-07-142521-7

Editorial and production services provided by CWL Publishing Enterprises, Inc., Madison, WI, www.cwlpub.com.

This book is printed on recycled, acid-free paper containing a minimum of 50% recycled de-inked fiber.

Contents

Chapter 1

Buying a House

1. How much can I afford to pay?

Borrowers often begin their home search with only the foggiest idea about how much they can afford to pay, which can result in wasted time and frustration. They should know approximately how much they can afford before they start to shop.

The amount you can spend on a house depends on your income, the amount of cash you can allocate to the transaction, and the mortgage terms available in the market at the time you are shopping. These include interest rates, points, term, down payment requirements, and the maximum allowable ratio of housing expense to income. In addition, affordability may be affected by your existing indebtedness, if this is higher than the indebtedness that lenders are willing to accept, and by closing costs, which vary from one part of the country to another.

To do it properly, affordability must be calculated three times, using three different rules. I call these the "income rule," the "debt rule," and the "cash rule." The final figure is the lowest of the three. When affordability is measured on the back of an envelope, which real estate brokers often do, usually it is based on the income rule alone, ignoring the other two. This can result in error.

The *income rule* says that the borrower's monthly housing expense (MHE)—which is the sum of the mortgage payment, property taxes and homeowner insurance premium—cannot exceed a percentage of e borrower's income specified by the lender. If this maximum is 28%, for example, and John Smith's monthly income is $4000, the MHE cannot exceed $1120. If taxes and insurance are $200, the maximum monthly mortgage payment is $920. At 7% and 30 years, this payment will support a loan of $138,282. Assuming a 5% down payment, this implies a sale price of $145,561. This is the maximum sale price for Smith using the income rule.

The *debt rule* says that the borrower's total housing expense (THE)—which is the sum of the MHE plus monthly payments on existing debt—cannot exceed a percentage of the borrower's income specified by the lender. If this maximum is 36%, for example, the THE for Smith cannot exceed $1440. If taxes and insurance are $200 and existing debt service is $240, the maximum mortgage payment is $1000. At 7% and 30 years, this payment will support a loan of $150,308. Assuming a 5% down payment, this implies a sale price of $158,218. This is the maximum sale price for Smith using the debt rule.

The *required cash rule* says that the borrower must have cash sufficient to meet the down payment requirement plus other settlement costs. If Smith has $12,000 and the sum of the down payment requirement and other settlement costs are 10% of the sale price, then the maximum sale price using the cash rule is $120,000. Since this is the lowest of the three maximums, it is the affordability estimate for Smith.

When the *cash rule* sets the limit on the maximum sale price, as in the case above, the borrower is said to be *cash constrained*. Affordability of a cash-constrained borrower can be raised by a reduction in the down payment requirement, a reduction in settlement costs, or access to an additional source of down payment—a parent, for example.

When the *income rule* sets the limit on the maximum sale price, the borrower is said to be *income constrained*. Affordability of an income-constrained borrower can be raised by a reduction in the maximum MHE ratio or access to additional income—sending a spouse out to work, for example.

When the *debt rule* sets the limit on the maximum sale price, the borrower is said to be *debt constrained*. The affordability of a debt-constrained borrower (but not that of a cash-constrained or income-constrained borrower) can be increased by repaying debt.

Affordability can be overestimated if one of the three rules is ignored and it turns out to be the one generating the lowest maximum price. The affordability estimate will also be affected by changes in the assumed maximum MHE and THE ratios, which vary from loan program to program and can also vary with other characteristics of the loan, such as the down payment. Affordability may also be affected by changes in the assumptions made regarding settlement costs, taxes and insurance, interest rate, and term.

You can see how any or all of these factors affect the amount you can afford using calculator 5a at www.mtg-professor.com.

2. How do lenders decide how much I can borrow?

From a lender's point of view, a "good loan" is one to a borrower who can demonstrate both the *ability* and the *willingness* to repay it. Qualification has to do with determining the borrower's ability to repay only. The borrower's willingness to repay is assessed largely by the applicant's past credit history. For a loan to be approved, the lender must be satisfied on both scores. This is the difference between "qualification" and "approval."

Lenders ask two basic questions about the borrower's ability to pay. First, is the borrower's income large enough to service the new expenses associated with the loan, plus any existing debt obligations that will continue in the future? Second, does the borrower have enough cash to meet the up-front cash requirements of the transaction? The lender must be satisfied on both counts.

In general, the lender assesses the adequacy of the borrower's income in terms of two ratios that have become standard in the trade. The first is called the *housing expense ratio*. It is the sum of the monthly mortgage payment including mortgage insurance, property taxes, and hazard insurance, divided by the borrower's monthly income. The second is called the *total expense ratio*. It is the same, except that the numerator includes the borrower's existing debt service obligations. For each of their loan programs, lenders set maximums for these ratios, such as 28% and 36%, which the actual ratios must not exceed.

Maximum expense ratios actually vary somewhat from one loan program to another. Hence, if you are only marginally over the limit, nothing more may be required than to find another program with higher maximum ratios. This is a situation where it is handy to be dealing with a mortgage broker who has access to loan programs of many lenders.

But even within one program, maximum expense ratios may vary with other characteristics of the transaction, and this can work against you. For example, the maximum ratios are often lower (more restrictive) for any of a long list of program "modifications," such as the property contains two to four separate dwelling units, the property is a co-op or a condominium or a second home or manufactured or designed for investment rather than owner occupancy, the borrower is self-employed, the loan is a cash-out refinance, and combinations of any of these.

The maximum ratios are not carved in stone if the borrower can make a persuasive case for raising them. The following are illustrative of circumstances where the limits may be waived.

- The borrower is just marginally over the housing expense ratio but well below the total expense ratio—29% and 30%, for example, when the maximums are 28% and 36%.

- The borrower has an impeccable credit record.
- The borrower is a first-time homebuyer who has been paying rent equal to 40% of income for three years and has an unblemished payment record.
- The borrower is making a large down payment.

If expense ratios exceed the maximums, one possible option is to reduce the mortgage payment by extending the term. If the term is already 30 years, however, there is very little that can be done. Few lenders offer 40-year loans and, anyway, extending the loan to 40 years doesn't reduce the mortgage payment much.

If you have planned to make a down payment larger than the absolute minimum, you can use the cash that would otherwise have gone to the down payment to reduce your expense ratios by paying off debt, paying points (points are fees the borrower pays the lender at the time the loan is closed) to reduce the interest rate, or funding a temporary buy-down.

The last is the most effective. With a temporary buy-down, which some lenders allow on some programs, cash is placed in an escrow account. An escrow account is a deposit account maintained by the lender and funded by the borrower, from which the lender makes tax and insurance payments for the borrower as they come due. But in this scenario, cash is also used to supplement a borrower's mortgage payments in the early years of the loan.

For example, on a 2-1 buy-down, the mortgage payment in years one and two are calculated at rates 2% and 1%, respectively, below the rate on the loan. The borrower makes these lower payments in the early years, which are supplemented by withdrawals from the escrow account. The expense ratios are lower because the payment used is the "bought-down" payment in the first month, rather than the total payment received by the lender.

Borrowers sometimes can obtain the additional cash required to reduce their expense ratios from family members, friends, and employers, but the most frequent contributors in the United States are home sellers, including builders. If the borrower is willing to pay the seller's price but cannot qualify, the cost to the seller of making the contribution the buyer needs to qualify may be less than the price reduction that would otherwise be needed to make the house saleable. (See "What is the down payment?" in Chapter 3.)

There may be circumstances where borrowers can change the income that the lenders use to qualify them for the loan. Lenders count only income that can be expected to continue, so they tend to disregard overtime, bonuses, and the like. The burden of proof is on the applicant to demonstrate that such other sources of income can indeed be expected to continue. The best way to do this is to show that they have in fact persisted over a considerable period in the past.

Borrowers who intend to share their house with another party can also consider the feasibility of making that party a co-borrower. In such case, the income used in the qualification process would include that of the co-borrower. Of course, the co-borrower would be equally responsible for repaying the loan. This works best when the relationship between the borrower and the co-borrower is permanent.

To qualify, applicants also need enough cash for the down payment and settlement costs. In the United States, however, mortgage insurance has substantially reduced down payment requirements. The quid pro quo is the mortgage insurance premium, which is like a higher interest rate.

On Federal Housing Administration (FHA) loans (see Chapter 4) and Veterans Administration (VA) loans, down payment requirements have been largely eliminated and all borrowers pay an insurance premium to the government. On conventional (not FHA or VA) loans, borrowers who put down less than 20% pay for private mortgage insurance. Premium categories are 15-19.99%, 10-14.99%, 5-9.99%, and 3-4.99%, with the premium rate highest for the last category.

In general, lenders want borrowers who put less than 20% down to meet the requirement with funds they have saved, as opposed to gifts from family and friends. Borrowers looking to parents for a major chunk of the down payment should make sure the money is in their own account several months before they apply for a loan. Funds borrowed for the down payment raise lender hackles even more, since they impose an additional repayment obligation on the borrower.

Recent years have seen the emergence of zero-down or 100% loans, as well as 107% and 125% loans. These loans carry higher interest rates rather than mortgage insurance premiums and they generally require that the borrower have excellent credit.

Chapter 2

Getting Qualified and Approved

3. What are the requirements for documenting income and assets?

The most important of the documentation requirements are as follows.

Full documentation: Both income and assets are disclosed and verified, and income is used in determining the applicant's ability to repay the mortgage. Formal verification requires the borrower's employer to verify employment and the borrower's bank to verify deposits. Alternative documentation, designed to save time, accepts copies of the borrower's original bank statements, W-2s, and paycheck stubs.

At one time, full documentation was the rule and it remains the standard. In recent years, however, other documentation programs have grown in importance.

Stated income, verified assets: Income is disclosed and the source of the income is verified, but the amount is not verified. Assets are verified and must meet an adequacy standard, such as, for example, six months of stated income and two months of expected monthly housing expense.

Stated income, stated assets: Both income and assets are disclosed but not verified. However, the source of the borrower's income is verified.

No ratio: Income is disclosed and verified but not used in qualifying the borrower. The standard rule that the borrower's housing expense cannot exceed some specified percent of income is ignored. Assets are disclosed and verified.

No income: Income is not disclosed, but assets are disclosed and verified and must meet an adequacy standard.

Stated assets or no asset verification: Assets are disclosed but not verified. Income is disclosed, verified, and used to qualify the applicant.

No assets: Assets are not disclosed, but income is disclosed, verified, and used to qualify the applicant.

No income, no assets: Neither income nor assets are disclosed.

While these categories are fairly well established in the market, there are numerous differences among individual lenders in the details. For example, under a stated income program, a lender may or may not require that an applicant sign a form authorizing the lender to request the applicant's tax returns from the IRS in the event the borrower defaults. Similarly, lenders differ in the amount of assets they require.

Why the proliferation of different documentation programs? Lenders have realized that many consumers with the potential for home ownership were shut out of the market by excessively rigid documentation requirements. It also dawned on lenders that documentation could be viewed as a risk factor that could be priced or offset by other risk factors. If a borrower has excellent credit and is putting 25% down, for example, why be so fussy about documentation?

Full documentation is the least risky to the lender, no income/no asset is the most risky, and the others are in between. If the documentation is riskier, lenders will charge more, require risk offsets, or both. The most important risk offsets are large down payments and high credit scores.

This change in lender attitudes toward documentation is similar to the change that occurred in connection with credit rating. At one time, lenders would deal only with what are today classified as "A-credit" borrowers. Now, loans are available for "B-," "C-," and "D-credit" borrowers, but they are priced higher and may require offsets by other risk factors.

The change in attitudes toward both credit rating and documentation requirements has expanded the market. Here are some examples of borrowers who would not have qualified under full documentation requirements:

- Jones is a personal trainer with no fixed place of business who makes good money but can't document it. He can document his mutual funds and his CPA can verify his self-employed status, so Jones qualifies under a stated income/verified assets plan.
- Smith is in the same business and uses the same CPA as Jones, but an uncle is gifting him with the cash he needs. Since Smith cannot document assets, he pays a little more under a stated income/stated asset program.
- King can document income and assets, but wants to allocate 58% of his income to housing expenses, which far exceeds conventional guidelines. King qualifies under a no-ratio loan.
- Queen is leaving her job to move to a new city where she has no job and will buy a house when she gets there with money from the sale of her current house. She has no income and cannot document assets because her old house won't be sold until after closing on the new one. Nevertheless, she qualifies under a no income/no asset program. If she has a contract of sale on the old house before closing on the new one, she will be able to document assets and can qualify under a no income program.

4. Can I improve my credit score by paying off delinquent credit cards?

Most everyone understands that if you don't pay your bills on time, your credit score suffers. There is a common misperception, however, that if you pay off these accounts, all will be forgiven—since the lender has been paid, the credit score will return to what it was before the delinquency. But it doesn't work that way.

Delinquencies reduce your credit score because the credit-scoring genie views delinquent accounts as evidence of a weak commitment toward meeting your obligations. The evidence is not wiped away when you repay the accounts. The delinquencies are still there, impacting your score. The only thing that will wipe them away is the passage of time and a better payment record.

A similar misperception is that consolidating credit card accounts into a smaller number of cards will improve the credit score. It will not if the consolidation of balances significantly raises the ratio of balances to available credit lines on the remaining cards. While the credit-scoring genie does not like a lot of cards, he likes even less a high ratio of loan balances to maximum available lines, because it may indicate financial distress.

If consolidation has reduced your credit score for that reason, don't try to undo the damage by opening more accounts. The genie has an especially strong distaste for multiple new accounts in a short period of time. That can be another indicator of financial distress.

Table 2-1 on the next page shows the best and the worst of credit card usage as seen by the genie who scores credit.

5. Will my credit score fall if I shop many loan providers?

Credit inquiries impact credit scores negatively because statistical studies show that multiple inquiries are associated with high risk of default. Distressed borrowers often contact many lenders hoping to find one who will approve them. On the other hand, multi-

Best	Worst
4 cards	15 cards
no delinquencies in past two years	many delinquencies in past two years
balance below 75% of line on all cards	many cards are maxed out
no cards acquired in last two years	three new cards acquired in last month

Table 2-1. Best and worst of credit card usage

ple inquiries can also result from applicants shopping for the best deal.

To avoid catching shoppers in his net, the genie who scores credit ignores inquiries that occur within 30 days of a score date. Suppose, for example, I shop a lender on May 30 and the lender has my credit scored that day. Even if I had shopped 50 other lenders in May and they had all checked my credit, none of those inquiries would affect my credit score on May 30.

Inquiries from April and back 11 months would, however, be counted on May 30. To avoid biasing the credit score from earlier shopping episodes, the scorers treat all inquiries that occur within any 14-day period as a single inquiry. If you shopped 50 lenders during April 1-14, they would count as one inquiry. If you spread them over April 1-28, they would count as two inquiries.

You will damage your credit if you spread your shopping over many months. But, because the market can change from day to day, it makes little sense to do this in any case.

Circumstances can cause a consumer to shop, drop out of the market, and return later when conditions are more favorable. You minimize the adverse effect by concentrating each shopping episode within 14 days or less.

6. Can you separate good income from bad credit?

Couples who purchase a home together often find that one of them has good credit and the other one has the income required to qualify. Lenders, however, are concerned with the credit of the borrower (or borrowers) whose income is being used to qualify. Good credit on the part of a borrower without the means to pay is of no use. Income and credit cannot be separated.

7. Is it difficult for the self-employed to qualify?

Some loan providers prefer not to deal with self-employed borrowers, because getting them qualified and approved is more complicated and onerous than with borrowers who work for a salary. But there are plenty of others that welcome business from the self-employed.

A major problem with lending to the self-employed is documenting an applicant's income to the lender's satisfaction. Applicants with jobs can provide lenders with pay stubs and lenders can verify the information by contacting the employer. With self-employed applicants, there are no third parties to verify such information.

Consequently, lenders fall back on income tax returns, which they typically require for two years. They feel safe in relying on income tax data, because any errors will be in the direction of understating rather than overstating income. Of course, they don't necessarily feel safe that the W-2s given them are authentic rather than concocted for the purpose of defrauding them, so they will require that the applicant authorize them to obtain copies directly from the IRS.

The second problem with lending to the self-employed is determining the stability of reported income. For this purpose, the lender wants to see an income statement for the period since the last tax return and, in some cases, a current balance sheet for the business.

The two government-sponsored enterprises that purchase enormous numbers of home loans in the secondary market, Federal National Mortgage Association (aka Fannie Mae) and Federal Home Loan Mortgage Corporation (aka Freddie Mac), have developed detailed guidelines for qualifying self-employed borrowers. Lenders looking to sell such loans to the agencies must follow the guidelines. The problem is that implementation can be complicated and time-consuming, especially when the declared income comes from a corporation or a partnership. If you own 25% or more, you are considered as "self-employed."

Most lenders offer "limited documentation" or "reduced documentation" loans to self-employed applicants who cannot demonstrate two years of sufficient income from their tax returns. These programs vary from lender to lender, but they all provide less favorable pricing and/or tougher underwriting requirements of other types. Lenders invariably require larger down payments, and may also require a better credit score or higher cash reserves. In addition, they may limit the types of properties or types of loans that are eligible.

The bottom line is that the system does service self-employed borrowers. While the hurdles are somewhat higher than they are for borrowers who work for third parties, the self-employed are also a highly resourceful group. If they can't get satisfaction from one mortgage broker or lender, they'll keep shopping until they find one who can meet their needs.

Chapter 3

Basic Mortgage Terms, Features, and Costs

8. What is a mortgage interest rate?

An interest rate is the price of money, and a mortgage interest rate is the price of money loaned against the security of a specific property. The interest rate is used to calculate the interest payment the borrower owes the lender.

The rates you see quoted are annual rates. On most home mortgages, the interest payment is calculated monthly. Hence, the rate is divided by 12 before calculating the payment.

Take a 6% rate, for example, and assume a $100,000 loan. In decimals, 6% is .06, and when divided by 12 it is .005. Multiple .005 times $100,000 and you get $500 as the monthly interest payment.

Suppose the borrower pays $600 this month. Then $500 of it covers the interest and $100 is used to reduce the balance. One month later, when another payment is due, the balance is $99,900, and the interest is $499.50. The interest rate stays the same, but the interest payment is lower because the balance is lower.

9. My loan officer says the total amount of interest I pay over the life of the loan is more important than the interest rate. Is this true?

No. The lower the interest rate you pay, the better off you are. But you can't say that about interest payments, which depend not only on the rate but also on the loan amount and the term. Reduce the loan amount and/or shorten the term and interest payments will fall. Whether either is in your interest depends on the circumstances. Reduce the loan amount and you need to come up with more cash for the down payment. Shorten the term and you have to make a larger monthly payment.

10. What are points and why should I pay them?

Points are fees the borrower pays the lender at the time the loan is closed, expressed as a percent of the loan. On a $100,000 loan, 3 points means a cash payment of $3,000. Points are part of the cost of credit to the borrower, and part of the investment return to the lender.

To my knowledge, points are only used in the United States. Borrowers need not pay points if they don't want to. While the quotations in the media usually include points, virtually all lenders are willing to make no-point loans if you ask for them. But of course the rate will be higher. The rate/point quotes you see in the media are what the lenders view as their "base" terms. But they have other rate/point combinations "in the drawer" to be trotted out when needed.

For example, a lender quoting 6.25% plus 2 points might also be offering 5.75% plus 4 points, 6.5% plus 0 points, and 7% plus a 1.5 point rebate or negative points.

Having these options is a positive feature of the U.S. system. The down side is that points add one more complexity to a process that is already complicated enough. The reason lenders usually keep all the combinations but one or two in the drawer is that they fear overwhelming the borrower—and perhaps losing the loan to another lender who makes it simpler.

Some borrowers have little or no leeway because they are "cash-short" or "income-short". If they are cash-short they are obliged to avoid points in order to have enough cash to complete the deal. If they are income-short, they must accept the lowest rate available so that the mortgage payment won't be viewed as excessive relative to their income.

If you have sufficient income and cash, you should be guided largely by your time horizon. If you expect to have the mortgage a long time, paying points to reduce the rate makes economic sense because you are going to enjoy the lower rate for a long time. If your time horizon is short, avoid points and pay the higher rate because you won't be paying it for long.

How long is "long"? This is shown for you in calculator 11a at www.decisionaide.com/mpcalculators/FRM BreakEvenCalculator/FRMBreakEven.asp and a companion calculator 11b applicable to adjustable-rate mortgages. Note that you may have a short horizon because you expect to move soon, or because you expect that interest rates will soon drop and you will be refinancing. I don't advise basing your estimated time horizon on interest rate expectations because you can't forecast interest rates.

11. Are points tax deductible?

The federal tax code treats points differently on purchase and refinance transactions. Points paid in cash on a purchase transaction are fully deductible in the year the loan is closed. If the points are included in the loan, however, they are not deductible as points. The loan amount will be higher, and therefore interest deductions will be greater, but these deductions are spread over the life of the loan. If you finance the points and repay early, much of the deduction derived from the points will be lost.

On a refinance, points paid in cash are deductible but the deduction must be spread evenly over the term. If the points were $3600 and the term was 30 years, for example, the deduction is just $10 a month! However, if you pay off the loan early, all unused deductions can be taken in the year of payoff. If the loan cited above is paid off after 5 years, for example, a deduction of $3,000 could be taken in the year of payoff.

Points on a refinance that are included in the loan are treated in the same way as points on a purchase that are included in the loan.

12. What is the down payment?

In dollars, the down payment is the difference between property value and loan amount. If value is $240,000 and the loan is $198,000, the down payment is $42,000.

In percent, the down payment is 1 minus the LTV—the ratio of loan to value. Since a loan of $198,000 is 82.5% of the value of $240,000, 1 - .825 is .175, or 17.5%. When the LTV is above 80%, the down payment is less than 20%, and the borrower must purchase mortgage insurance.

The down payment is often confused with the amount of cash the borrower puts into the transaction. In fact, the down payment is smaller because of settlement costs. For example, if you have $48,000 in cash and purchase a $240,000 house, your cash would be 20% of value. But if settlement costs are $5,000, you are left with only $43,000 for the down payment.

13. If a house is appraised for more than the sale price, can the difference be counted as part of the down payment?

No. The rule is that the property value used in determining the down payment and the LTV is the sale price or appraised value, *whichever is lower.* The only exception to this is when the seller provides a gift of equity to the buyer, who is almost always a family member. In this case, the lender recognizes that the house is being priced below market and will accept the appraisal as the value. Most lenders in such cases will require two appraisals, and they will take the lower of the two.

14. Can the seller help with the down payment?

No, but seller contributions can be used to pay the borrower's settlement costs, provided that it is disclosed to the lender. That is just as good as contributing to the down payment, since cash that the borrower would otherwise have to use to pay settlement costs is now available for the down payment. For this to work, the appraiser must say that the house is worth the higher price.

For example, Jones offers his house to Smith for $200,000, which Smith is willing to pay. But under the best financing terms available to Smith, he needs $12,000, which he doesn't have. This is shown in the "Before" column of the table on the next page.

So Jones and Smith agree that Jones will raise the price of the house to $206,000 and Jones will gift Smith $6,000. Assuming the appraiser goes along, the amount of cash required of Smith drops from $12,000 to $6,360, making the purchase affordable. Jones gets his price and Smith gets his house, so everyone is happy—except, perhaps, the lender.

Appraisals often ratify sale prices, whether justified or not. If the house is actually only worth the original offer price of $200,000, the buyer has only $180 of real equity—the difference between the original property value and the higher loan amount—rather than $6,180. Less equity means greater loss for the lender if the loan goes into default.

	Before	After
Sale Price	$200,000	$206,000
Appraised Value		$206,000
Loan Amount	$194,000	$199,820
Down Payment (3%)	$6,000	$6,180
Total Cash Required	$12,000	$6,360
Down Payment (3%)	$6,000	$6,180
Settlement Costs (3%)	$6,000	$6,180
Gift From Seller	0	$6,000
Buyer's Stated Equity	$6,000	$6,180
Buyer's Real Equity	$6-12,000	$180-6,180

Table 3-1. Getting help from the seller

For this reason, lenders and mortgage insurers limit seller contributions to buyers. The smaller the down payment requirement, the more critical the issue becomes. On conventional loans (loans not insured by the federal government), it is common to restrict seller contributions to 3% of sale price with 5% down, and to 6% with 10% down. On FHA loans, sellers can contribute up to 6% of price to the buyer's settlement costs, but nothing to the down payment.

15. What is the real cost of mortgage insurance?

Lenders require mortgage insurance on any loan that exceeds 80% of property value. The larger the loan relative to value, the higher the insurance premium. While the insurance premium is assessed against the entire loan, the cost should be allocated entirely to the portion of the loan that exceeds 80% of value.

Assume I can obtain a 30-year fixed rate mortgage at 7.5% and zero points to purchase a $100,000 house.

Without mortgage insurance, I could borrow up to $80,000 (80% of property value), whereas with mortgage insurance I could borrow up to $95,000 (95% of property value). The insurance premium on the $95,000 loan is .79% of the balance per year for the first 10 years, after which it drops to .20%.

The best approach to measuring the cost of the insurance premium is to view the loan of $95,000 as consisting of two loans: one for $80,000, which has an interest cost of 7.5% consisting solely of the interest rate; and one for $15,000, the cost of which includes both the interest rate and the insurance premium. The interest cost on the $15,000 loan turns out to be 12.7% if you stay in your house for up to 10 years, declining slowly after that to 12% if you stay a full 30 years.

Since the insurance premium is only .79%, how can the cost of the $15,000 loan be 5.2% higher than the cost of the $80,000 loan? The reason is that while you are borrowing an additional $15,000, you pay the premium on the entire $95,000.

The cost calculation above assumes that you take a fixed-rate mortgage with a loan-to-value ratio of 95%, and pay mortgage insurance for 10 years. Change the assumptions and you change the cost. For example, on 85% and 90% loans, the cost is 13.4% and 12.5%, respectively. While the insurance premiums are smaller, the incremental loans are also smaller.

On smaller loans within the same mortgage insurance premium bracket, the cost is higher. For example, the cost of insurance on a 91% fixed-rate loan, which has the same premium as a 95% loan, is 14.3%.

Adjustable rate mortgages have higher insurance premiums, and therefore higher costs, than fixed-rate mortgages.

Mortgage insurance costs can be reduced if you manage to get the insurance removed early. For example, if the insurance on a 95% fixed-rate mortgage is removed in five years but you stay with the mortgage for 10, the cost falls to 10.8%. However, if you move in five years and pay off the mortgage, there is no saving.

Here is a handy rule-of-thumb for estimating the interest cost on the incremental loan made possible by mortgage insurance, assuming the loan runs 10 years. Divide the total loan by the incremental loan and multiply the result by the annual insurance premium, e.g., $95,000 divided by $15,000 equals $6.33, which when multiplied by .79% equals 5%. Adding that to the interest rate gives an estimated cost of 12.5% on the incremental $15,000 loan.

The choice between a smaller loan without insurance and a larger loan with insurance can be viewed as an investment decision. Taking the smaller loan means investing $15,000 in a larger down payment that provides a risk free return of 12.5%. Is this an attractive investment?

Not if you don't have the $15,000. Even if you have it, you would be locking it up for an indefinite period, although you might borrow against it using a home equity loan. Or you may not be impressed with a 12.5% return if you can earn more than that in your business, or are paying more on credit card loans. On the other hand, if you have a bond portfolio earning 7%, you might well want to liquidate it to invest in the larger down payment.

16. How can I avoid private mortgage insurance?

In addition to putting 20% down, there are two other ways to avoid purchasing private mortgage insurance (PMI). One way is to pay a higher interest rate in lieu of PMI. When a borrower accepts this option, the lender buys PMI for less than the borrower would have to pay. The higher interest rate covers the insurance cost to the lender plus a profit margin. Some but not all lenders offer this option.

The sales pitch for the higher rate as a replacement for PMI is that interest is tax deductible whereas PMI premiums are not. The other side of the coin, however, is that you must pay the higher interest for the life of your mortgage, while mortgage insurance will be terminated at some point.

On most loans closed after July 29, 1999, mortgage insurance must be cancelled at the borrower's request if the loan balance is paid down to 80 percent of the original property value. Further, insurance must be terminated automatically when the balance reaches 78% of the original value. In addition, subject to certain conditions, PMI on loans sold by lenders to the two federal agencies (Fannie Mae and Freddie Mac) must be cancelled when the loan balance reaches 80% of the *current* property value, taking account of appreciation.

In general, if you expect significant appreciation and monitor your property value so you can terminate PMI as soon as possible, the higher interest rate option is a poor choice—unless you expect to hold the mortgage a very short time. In other cases, it could be a good choice.

You can use calculator 14a at www.mtgprofessor.com to determine whether the higher rate or PMI results in a lower cost in your particular case.

The second way to avoid paying for PMI is to take a first mortgage for 80% of value, and a second mortgage for 10% or 15%. These are known as 80/10/10s and 80/15/5s, where the last number is the down payment.

In general, combination loans are more attractive the higher your tax bracket, the smaller the difference in rate between the two mortgages, and the shorter the term of the higher-rate second. Expected rapid price appreciation reduces the attractiveness of combination loans because it means that mortgage insurance will terminate sooner.

Calculator 13a at www.mtgprofessor.com pulls together these and other relevant factors, calculating the costs of both options over the period you expect to be in your house. It also shows the "break-even rate" on the second mortgage, which is the highest rate it makes sense to pay. The combination will save you money if the market rate on the second is below the break-even rate.

17. Why do I need title insurance?

If you need a mortgage, you must purchase title insurance because all mortgage lenders require it, for an amount equal to the loan. It lasts until the loan is repaid. As with mortgage insurance, you pay the premium, which is a single-payment made upfront. Title insurance protects against loss arising from problems connected to the title to your property. Before you purchased your home, it may have gone through several ownership changes, and the land on which it stands went through many more. There may be a weak link at any point in that chain that could emerge to cause trouble. For example, someone along the way may have forged a signature in transferring title. Or there may be unpaid real estate taxes or other liens. Title insurance covers the insured party for any claims and legal fees that arise out of such problems.

Title insurance protects against losses arising from events that occurred *prior* to the date of the policy. Coverage ends on the day the policy is issued and extends backward in time for an indefinite period. This is in marked contrast to property or life insurance, which protect against losses resulting from events that occur *after* the policy is issued, for a specified period into the future.

18. Does title insurance protect me or the lender?

The title insurance required by the lender protects the lender up to the amount of the mortgage, but it doesn't protect your equity in the property. For that you need an owner's title policy for the full value of the home. In many areas, sellers pay for owner policies as part of their obligation to deliver good title to the buyer. In other areas, borrowers must buy it as an add-on to the lender policy. It is advisable to do this because the additional cost above the cost of the lender policy is relatively small.

Protection under an owner's policy lasts as long as the owner or any heirs have an interest in or any obligation with regard to the property. When they sell, however, the lender will require the purchaser to obtain a new policy. That protects the lender against any liens or other claims against the property that may have arisen since the date of the previous policy.

For example, if the contractor you failed to pay for remodeling your kitchen places a lien on your home, you are not protected by your title policy; the lien was placed after the date of the policy. You will probably be required to get the lien removed before you can sell the property. But in the event the lien hasn't been removed and a search has failed to uncover it, the new lender will be protected by a new policy.

19. Can I shop around for title insurance?

Yes, unlike mortgage insurance, where the carrier is always selected by the lender, borrowers can select the title insurance carrier. Few do, however. Most leave it up to one of the professionals with whom they deal—real estate agent, lender or attorney. This means that competition among title insurers is largely directed toward these professionals who can direct business rather than toward borrowers.

20. Does it pay to shop around?

Perhaps. It is difficult to generalize because market conditions vary state by state, and sometimes within states.

I would certainly shop in states that do not regulate title insurance rates: Alabama, District of Columbia,

Georgia, Hawaii, Illinois, Indiana, Massachusetts, Oklahoma, and West Virginia.

You would be wasting your time shopping in Texas and New Mexico, because these state set the prices for all carriers. Florida also sets title insurance premiums but not other title-related charges, which can vary.

In the remaining states, the situation is murky and it may or may not pay to shop. Insurance premiums are the same for all carriers in "rating bureau states": Pennsylvania, New York, New Jersey, Ohio, and Delaware. These states authorize title insurers to file for approval of a single rate schedule for all carriers through a cooperative entity. Yet in some there may be flexibility in title-related charges. More promising are "file and use" states—all those not mentioned above—that permit premiums to vary between insurers.

It is a good idea to ask an informed but disinterested person whether it pays to shop in the area where the property is located. Just keep in mind that those likely to be the best informed are also likely to have an interest in directing your business in the direction that is most advantageous to them.

Chapter 4

The Different Types of Mortgages

21. Which is preferable, a 30-year term or a 15-year term?

If you cannot afford the monthly payment on a 15-year loan, your choice is made for you. If you can afford the 15, you must decide whether you are a *payment-minimizer* or *wealth-maximizer.* The first group is concerned mainly with the present, the second with the future.

The mortgage payment on a $100,000 30-year loan at 7% is $665 while on a 15-year loan at 6.75% it is $885. The payment minimizer is drawn to the lower payment on the 30.

On the other hand, after 5 years the borrower who took out the 15-year loan has repaid $22,933 while the borrower who took out the 30 has repaid only $5,868. That amounts to a difference in wealth accumulation of $17,065. To me, that's even more attractive; I'm a wealth-maximizer.

Some borrowers who can afford the 15 opt for the 30 because of the flexibility it provides. You can make the larger payment of the 15, they argue, but you don't have to; if you get into a pinch, you can make the lower payment of the 30. Those who take a 30 but make the larger payment of the 15, however, don't pay down the balance as rapidly as they would have if they had taken a 15 because they are paying the higher rate of the 30.

I have found that many borrowers who elect the 30-year option to obtain flexibility subsequently find that they really don't want it after all! After a few years of being homeowners, they discover that what they really want is to build equity more quickly than the 30 allows. They discover, in other words, that they want to build wealth.

At that point some of those who took out 30-year loans begin systematically making additional monthly payments in order to build equity faster. Of course, they would have been better off taking the 15-year at the outset and enjoying the lower interest rate, but better late than never.

If the rates on the 30 and 15 are 7% and 6.75%, for example, a 10% investment yield would not put you ahead for 63 months. At investment yields of 12%, 14%, and 16%, the periods are 41, 30 and 24 months, respectively. If the rate on the 15 is 6.5%, the periods are almost twice as long.

22. How are interest rates determined on an adjustable rate mortgage (ARM)?

There are two phases in the life of an adjustable rate mortgage (ARM). During the first phase, the interest rate is fixed, just as it is on a fixed rate mortgage (FRM). The difference is that on an FRM the rate is fixed for the term of the loan, whereas on an ARM it is fixed for a shorter period. The period ranges from one month to 10 years.

At the end of the initial rate period, the ARM rate is adjusted. The adjustment rule is that the new rate will equal the most recent value of a specified interest rate index, plus a margin. (The margin is specified in the note and remains unchanged through the life of the ARM.) For example, if the index is 5% when the initial rate period ends, and the margin is 2.75%, the new rate will be 7.75%. The rule, however, is subject to two conditions.

The first condition is that the increase from the previous rate cannot exceed any rate adjustment cap specified in the ARM contract. An adjustment cap, usually 1% or 2% but ranging in some cases up to 5%, limits the size of any interest rate change.

The second condition is that the new rate cannot exceed the contractual maximum rate. Maximum rates are usually 5 or 6 percentage points above the initial rate.

During the second phase of an ARM's life, the interest rate is adjusted periodically. This period may or may not be the same as the initial rate period. For example, an ARM with an initial rate period of 5 years might adjust annually after the 5-year period ends. It is referred to as a "5/1 ARM." There are also 3/1, 7/1 and 10/1 ARMs. In some cases, the second adjustment period could be a month.

The rate that is quoted on an ARM, by the media and by loan providers, is the initial rate—regardless of how long that rate lasts. When the initial rate period is short, the quoted rate is a poor indication of interest cost to the borrower. The only significance of the initial rate on a monthly ARM, for example, is that this rate may be used to calculate the initial payment.

The index plus margin is called the "fully-indexed rate" (FIR). The FIR based on the most recent value of the index at the time the loan is taken out indicates where the ARM rate may go when the initial rate period ends. If the index rate does not change, the FIR will become the ARM rate.

For example, assume the initial rate is 4% for 1 year, the fully indexed rate is 7%, and the rate adjusts every year subject to a 1% rate increase cap. If the index value remains the same, the 7% FIR will be reached at the end of the third year.

23. Can you have peace of mind with an ARM?

The worst thing about the adjustable rate mortgages (ARMs) we have in the U.S. is not that they are so dangerous but that they are so complicated. Ironically, the complications arise primarily out of efforts to make them less dangerous.

ARMs in the U.S. differ from ARMs that are the standard instrument in most other countries in three major ways:

1. *The initial period during which the rate is preset is longer.* In South Africa, some banks offer "fixed-rate" mortgages, by which they mean that the initial rate can last as long as 2 years before lender discretion kicks in! In the U.S., initial rate periods run as long as 10 years.
2. *Rate adjustments are automated.* Rate adjustments on ARMs in the United States are determined not by the board of directors of the lending institution but by a computer that has been programmed to apply a set of adjustment rules that are stipulated in the ARM contract. The central rule is that the rate will be adjusted on pre-specified dates to equal the value on that date of an interest rate index over which the lender has no control. The lender has zero discretion.
3. *Rate adjustments are generally constrained.* The great majority of ARMs in the U.S. limit rate changes on any one adjustment date ("adjustment caps") and also set a maximum rate over the life of the instrument ("lifetime cap"). There are some that have only adjustment caps, and some with only lifetime caps, but very few have neither.

These important features of ARMs in the United States protect consumers but they also befuddle them. The educational materials on ARMs that the government requires lenders to provide to borrowers are not much help. Even those who master these materials have great difficulty bringing them to bear on the specific ARMs they are being offered. And many borrowers want to protect themselves without having to learn a lot of boring stuff for which they will have no later use.

One way to meet this problem is by using calculators 9a or 9b at www.mtgprofessor.com to determine when and by how much your future payments might rise. Peace of mind comes from knowing that you will be able to deal with the payment changes that will come from the worst scenario you can imagine.

24. How do balloon loans compare with ARMs?

Balloon loans are payable in full after a period that is shorter than the term. In the 1920s most balloon loans were interest-only—the borrower paid interest but no principal. At maturity, usually 5 or 10 years, the balloon that had to be repaid was equal to the original loan amount. Most balloon loans offered today, in contrast, calculate payments on a 30-year amortization schedule, so there is some principal reduction. Assuming a rate of 6.5%, for example, a $100,000 loan would have a balance remaining at the end of the fifth year of $93,611. The interest-only variant has reappeared, however.

Borrowers often choose between a 5-year balloon loan and a 5/1 ARM, or between a 7-year balloon loan and a 7 /1 ARM. Both offer a rate in the early years below that available on a 30-year fixed-rate mortgage, and both carry a risk of higher rates later on. But there are some important differences.

Favoring the balloon:

- Balloon loans are much simpler to understand, and therefore easier to shop for.
- The interest rate on a 5-year or 7-year balloon is typically lower than that on a 5/1 or 7/1 ARM.

Favoring the ARM:

- The risk of a substantial rate increase after 5 or 7 years is greater on the balloon. The balloon must be refinanced at the prevailing market rate, whereas a rate increase on most 5 and 7-year ARMs is limited by rate caps.
- Borrowers with 5-year balloons incur refinancing costs at term, whereas borrowers with 5/1 ARMs don't unless they elect to refinance.
- Borrowers who are having payment problems may find it difficult to refinance balloons. The balloon contract allows lenders to decline to refinance if the borrower has missed a single payment in the prior year. This is not a problem with ARMs, which need not be refinanced.
- Borrowers may find it difficult to refinance balloons if interest rates have spiked. The balloon contract allows lenders to decline to refinance if current market rates are more than 5% higher than the rate on the balloon.

25. Should I get a biweekly mortgage to pay off the loan early?

With a biweekly mortgage, you pay half the monthly payment every 2 weeks, which results in an extra monthly payment every year. (Twenty-six payments, each one for half of one monthly payment, is the equivalent of 13 monthly payments rather than 12). Because of the extra payment, a biweekly mortgage pays off early.

The biweekly mortgage dazzles a lot of people because they confuse the interest payments over the life of the loan with the interest rate. Total interest payments paid over the life of a loan depend on the rate, on the amount borrowed, and on how rapidly the loan is paid off. Converting a conventional loan to a biweekly does not change the interest rate. What it does is to use the extra payment you make every year to reduce the balance, which in turn reduces interest payments. The loan is paid off early, just as it would have been if you had begun with a mortgage carrying a shorter term.

In fact, borrowers taking out a new loan who are attracted to the accelerated repayment schedule on a biweekly, are usually better off with a conventional loan having a shorter term. For example, 15 and 20-year loans often carry lower rates than 30-year loans, whereas a borrower taking a 30-year biweekly will pay the 30-year rate, even though a 7% biweekly pays off in about 23 years.

If you already have a 30-year mortgage and are attracted by the prospect of paying it off early, there is nothing wrong with converting it to a biweekly, but it will cost you. No one is going to do the work of converting your existing loan into a biweekly without being compensated. The main compensation may be the earnings on the money you deposit over the two weeks prior to the monthly payment to the lender, which is not an out-of-pocket cost to you. But it is an "opportunity" cost in the sense that you would have had those earnings if you had not elected to convert.

There are alternatives that cost nothing. If you regularly receive a bonus at the end of the year, for example, adopt the practice of sending your lender an additional check equal to the amount of the bonus, marked "partial prepayment", along with your regular check for the monthly payment. Note: if you make an extra payment equal to your regular monthly payment at the end of each year, you will pay off the balance just as you would with a biweekly.

Another approach is simply to increase your current monthly payment. If you divide your monthly payment by 12, and add that amount to your payment every month, you will actually pay off the loan sooner than if you convert to a biweekly. You start reducing the balance (and interest on that balance) with the first additional payment, whereas with a biweekly it takes a year before you begin reducing the balance.

These alternative approaches require self-discipline on your part, which you may or may not be able to manage. Having a third party set up the procedure and then legally obligating yourself to make the additional payments forces the discipline upon you. In the last analysis, this discipline is the only service you receive when you purchase a biweekly deal from a third party. Whether you need it only you can decide.

26. Who should take a Federal Housing Adminstration (FHA) loan?

FHA loans are for borrowers who seek loans no larger than the loan size limits set by the FHA program, and either can't meet a 3% down payment requirement, have poor credit, or both. FHA loan size limits vary by county, are reset every year, and can be found at https://entp.hud.gov/idapp/html/hicostlook.cfm. Second mortgages are prohibited with the FHA loan.

Most FHA borrowers make down payments of less than 3 percent. FHA allows you to buy a home with 1% down. Private mortgage insurers require 5 percent down on most loans, and only allow 3 percent down on special programs. FHA is also liberal in allowing gifts to be used for paying settlement costs.

FHA borrowers also usually have weaker credit than private insurers accept. FHA allows higher ratios of expense to income, is more tolerant of existing debt, and will allow the income of co-borrowers who don't live in the house to count fully in measuring income adequacy. It is also quite forgiving about bad credit. For example, a borrower need be out of a Chapter 7 bankruptcy for only 2 years, and out of a Chapter 13 bankruptcy for only 1 year.

But there is a third group of FHA borrowers that shouldn't exist. It is comprised of borrowers who meet the requirements of a conventional loan but are steered to an FHA. This happens because loan officers who specialize in FHAs don't like to lose a customer.

FHA loans are generally available in the market at about the same interest rate and points as conventional loans with the same term. There may be a difference in mortgage insurance premiums, however.

On an FHA 30-year fixed-rate mortgage (FRM), the mortgage insurance premium is 1.5% of the loan amount paid up front plus .5% of the loan balance paid monthly. The premium is the same regardless of the down payment.

On conventional loans, the insurance premium depends on the down payment. With 5% down, the premium on a 30-year FRM is about the same as on an FHA. With 10% or more down, the premium on conventional loans is lower. Borrowers who can put 10% down and have good credit will usually do better with a conventional loan.

Recently, an additional option has opened for borrowers who are unable to make a down payment but have strong credit. The interest rate is higher on these zero-down-loans, but you don't have to pay for mortgage insurance. When I compared, the best deal I could find on the Internet on an FHA 30-year FRM with the comparable zero-down loan offered on-line by Countrywide Funding, the total cost of the latter was lower. Cash-poor borrowers with good credit should explore this new option.

Chapter 5

How to Understand Mortgage Pricing

27. What is the price of a mortgage loan?

One complication of mortgages is that their "price" has at least three components. ARMs have even more.

Interest rate is the number that is multiplied by the loan balance to get the interest payment due the lender. The rate quoted on a mortgage is an annual rate, but it is applied monthly. On a 6% mortgage with a $100,000 balance, for example, the monthly interest due is .005 times $100,000, or $500.

On a fixed-rate mortgage (FRM), the interest rate is preset for the life of the loan. On an adjustable-rate mortgage (ARM), the rate is preset for an initial period, ranging from one month to 10 years, and then can change.

Points are up-front charges expressed as a percent of the loan amount. Two points amount to 2% of the loan.

Points are related to the interest rate. If a lender offers a 30-year FRM at 8% and zero points, for example, he might charge 1.75 points for a 7.5% loan.

Rebates are points paid by the lender for high-rate loans. The lender who charges 1.75 points for a 7.5% loan, for example, might rebate 2 points for a 9% loan. The 2 points would be available to defray the borrower's settlement costs.

Origination fees are points in disguise. Some lenders charge origination fees because reporting services and newspapers show rates and points but not origination fees. The lender who charges 1 point and a 1% origination fee looks cheaper than the lender who charges 2 points and no origination fee. To the borrower, points and origination fees are the same.

"Junk fees" is a nasty term sometimes used to describe all other up-front charges by the lender or mortgage broker. Junk fees are expressed in dollars rather than as a percent of the loan. At www.mtgprofessor.com I have a long list of items that some lenders may charge for, but for the borrower shopping the market, only the total matters.

In sum, the price of a fixed-rate mortgage has three components: interest rate, total up-front charges expressed as a percent of the loan, and total up-front charges expressed in dollars.

ARM shoppers who confidently expect to be out of the house before the end of the initial rate period need concern themselves only with the initial rate. But ARM shoppers who are uncertain about how long they will be in their house should have two indicators of what might happen to the ARM rate after the initial rate period ends.

The *fully indexed rate* (FIR) tells them where the ARM rate will go in a stable interest rate environment. The FIR is the sum of the interest rate index used by the ARM and the fixed *margin* that is added to it. Both the index and the margin are specified in the ARM contract. At the end of the initial rate period, assuming the interest rate index does not change from its initial value, the rate on the ARM will move toward the FIR.

The *maximum rate* tells them where the ARM rate will go in a rising rate environment. It is the highest rate permitted by the ARM contract. Even if interest rates explode, the ARM rate cannot exceed this maximum.

It is also useful for an ARM shopper to know whether rate adjustments at the end of the initial rate period will be abrupt or gradual. This depends on how frequently rates are adjusted and on the cap (if any) on how large a rate adjustment can be.

28. What market niche are you in?

Market nichification is a unique feature of the U.S. mortgage system that complicates life for mortgage shoppers. Nichification means that lenders vary the terms they offer borrowers based on a large number of loan, borrower, and property characteristics that they believe affect the risk or cost of the loan to them.

For example, lenders consider loans that are used to purchase a property for investment riskier than loans used to purchase a property that will be occupied as a residence by the borrower. To compensate lenders for the risk, loans for investment carry a rate about 0.75% higher than the rate on loans for personal occupancy. In addition, the maximum amount you can borrow on an investor loan is about 70% of property value, as opposed to 95% on most loans for occupancy.

Here are some other examples of nichification:

- A $400,000 loan costs more than a $300,000 loan.
- A 30-year loan costs more than a 15.
- A zero-down payment loan costs more than a loan with a down payment.
- A loan on which the price is locked for 60 days costs more than one locked for only 30 days.
- A loan on a two-family house or a condominium costs more than a loan on a single-family house.
- A loan to refinance costs more than a loan to purchase a house.
- A loan to refinance with cash-out costs more than a refinance with no cash-out.
- A loan on a vacation home costs more than one on a primary residence.

- A loan with simplified or no documentation requirements costs more than a loan with conventional documentation.
- A loan where one co-borrower is a non-occupant costs more than a loan where all co-borrowers occupy the house.
- A loan to a borrower with poor credit costs more than a loan to a borrower with good credit.

But a list such as this oversimplifies, because many of the factors affecting price have more than two options. For example, at one time credit was either OK or not OK, but today credit is scaled more like a report card; it might be A, A-, B, C, D, and F. Similarly, documentation requirements have grown from two (conventional and simplified) to at least eight.

Because of niche combinations, the total number of niches is enormous. Six credit categories and eight documentation categories result in 48 niches for just these two factors alone. Software developed by GHR Systems, Inc., which many major lenders use to make pricing adjustments, allows lenders to enter up to *40 million prices for each loan program*. What does nichification mean for shoppers?

First, they need to understand that no lender operates in every niche, and the narrower the niche, the fewer the lenders. This is a major reason for patronizing mortgage brokers. Since mortgage brokers deal with multiple lenders, often 30 or more, they are well positioned (as consumers are not) to identify the lenders who operate in a particular niche and select the best of the available deals.

Second, shoppers need to locate themselves in the correct market niche before they solicit price quotes from loan providers. Otherwise, they don't know whether the price information collected reflects correct niche pricing or not. One of the advantages of shopping on-line is that the better on-line Web sites query users about the loan, property, and finances in order to provide the correct niche pricing. If you are in a really exotic niche, they won't catch it, but most users will be priced correctly.

Third, shoppers need to understand that the lender offering the best deal in one niche is not necessarily the one offering the best deal in another niche. In a study that I did some time ago of 13 lenders operating in 19 niches, 12 of them offered the best deal in at least one niche and no one lender offered the best deal in more than three of the 19 niches.

Finally, shoppers should be wary of shifting niches after they lock the price. Suppose you are locked, but 10 days before settlement you decide you want to change your niche. Perhaps you originally selected a 30-year loan and now you want a 15 or maybe you want to pay more points to reduce the interest rate. The price of the new loan should be based on the prices existing at the time the original prices were locked, but you won't know what those were. And since you have a closing in 10 days and have nowhere to go, the loan officer may be tempted to earn a few more dollars at your expense. For example, he or she may reduce your interest rate on the 15-year by by 3/8% instead of the 1/2% difference instead of the difference on the original price sheet. For this reason, it is a good idea to request a range of rate/point quotations on the lock date, for each of the mortgage types you might conceivably decide you want.

29. Can I rely on price quotes in the printed media?

In general, you can't rely on a price quote from any source until a lender locks the price of your specific deal. This usually requires that you have submitted an application.

Price quotes in the printed media do not deal adequately with market nichification. (See the preceding question, "What Market Niche Are You In?") Media quotes assume, among other things, that you have good

credit, have sufficient income and assets to meet the lender's requirements, can fully document your income and assets, are purchasing a single-family detached house that all co-borrowers will occupy as their primary residence, and will not have a second mortgage on the house when the loan closes. If you don't meet all of these specifications, the quoted prices don't apply.

Price quotes in the printed media also cannot deal adequately with market volatility. Most mortgage lenders change their prices daily, generally in the morning after secondary markets open, and sometimes they will change them during the day as well. This means that a newspaper that publishes price information in its Monday edition is reporting Friday's prices. On Monday, when the paper hits the street, lenders have already posted new prices.

Other limitations of the printed media are that they report interest rate and points only, ignoring the fixed-dollar fees charged by lenders; on ARMs, they show the initial interest rate and period only, ignoring the margin and other important components of the ARM price; and they do not report prepayment penalties.

While price information in the printed media is largely worthless, this is not the case with information on the Internet. For example, some sites adjust prices at least partially for the user's market niche and keep prices current at all times.

30. Can I rely on price quotes received directly from a loan provider?

It depends on the loan provider. But if one quotes a price significantly better than all the others, you can assume that it is phony—meaning that the lender or broker has no intention of honoring it.

What's the point? To rope you in.

If you are purchasing a house, the cost of terminat-

ing the process with one loan provider and starting again with another becomes increasingly high as you move toward your home closing date. As your bargaining power recedes with the passage of time, you become increasingly vulnerable to various tricks for increasing the price.

Loan providers who offer phony quotes figure that once you are in the application process they have a good chance of landing you as a borrower.

I know a mortgage broker who aims to make a 1.5-point markup on all loans (each point is 1% of the loan amount), but includes only a 0.5 point markup on prices he quotes over the telephone. For example, if this broker has a quote from a wholesale lender of 8.25% and 1 point, he quotes you 8.25% and 1.5 points—a markup of only 0.5 points. If he lands you as a customer, he finds a way to recover the point (or more) before the loan terms are locked.

Brokers who practice this deceit are called "sunshine blowers" by those that don't.

How do they get away with it? Loan providers legally can't be held to a price quote. Since the market is volatile, yesterday's price may not apply today. All loan providers, including the sunshine blowers, warn borrowers that price quotes aren't firm until they are locked.

For example, suppose market interest rates rise after the initial quote, so the original wholesale quote of 8.25% and 1 point now go to 8.25% and 1.5 points. The broker tells you, "Sorry, the market has gone against us; the loan you want is now at 8.25% and 3 points." The broker makes an extra point and a half by pretending that the increase in market rates was larger than it was.

Conversely, if the wholesale quote falls to 8.25% and zero points, the broker can make his 1.5-point markup by providing you with the terms originally quoted. The broker merely ignores the decline in market rates.

You can attempt to forestall this trickery by monitoring changes in the market after you get a price quote, but probably you won't get far.

The broker will point out that your market information is general and does not accurately describe the specific segment of the market relevant to your loan. Only the broker has *that* information. You will probably lose this argument, because you're fighting on the broker's turf and you have a closing date on the near horizon.

It would be a different story if the broker agreed initially to share his or her market information with you. If the broker in my example revealed the wholesale lenders' price quotes, you would know exactly how the market relevant to you had changed. But then the broker would not be able to modify his low-ball markup, which is one reason most brokers keep wholesale prices to themselves. But an upfront mortgage broker will share his or her wholesale prices with you. (See Chapter 6, "What is an upfront mortgage broker?")

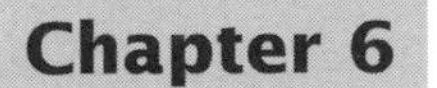

Shopping for Your Mortgage

31. How do I shop for the lowest-cost mortgage?

The best approach to settlement costs depends on whether you are dealing with a lender or with a mortgage broker. I'll deal with the lender case first.

Settlement costs can be divided into the following categories:

1. Lender fees
2. Lender-controlled fees paid to third parties
3. Other fees paid to third parties
4. Other settlement costs

Lender fees should be the shopper's major focus. Lender fees consist of points and "dollar fees" (aka "junk fees").

Points are an up-front charge expressed as a percent of the loan amount, such as "one point" or "two points," meaning "1% of the loan" or "2% of the loan." An origination fee, as I said earlier ("What is the price of a mortgage loan?" in Chapter 5) is points in disguise: it is the same as points, except it is not related to the interest rate.

Dollar fees are fees specified in dollars, such as fees for processing, tax service, flood certification, underwriting, wire transfer, document preparation, courier, and lender inspection.

But from a shopping perspective, what they are

called doesn't matter and whether they are justified doesn't matter. All that matters, for the purposes of your negotiation with the lender, is the sum total of these fees.

Shoppers typically pay close attention to points in selecting a lender because lenders always report points alongside the interest rate. Dollar fees and origination fees, however, are not reported in the media and generally are not volunteered by lenders. For this reason, shoppers often fail to consider them when selecting a lender.

Shoppers should ask for dollar fees and should expect the lender to guarantee them through to closing. In contrast to guaranteeing a rate and points, which exposes a lender to market risks, there is virtually no risk in guaranteeing dollar fees. The same is true of an origination fee.

Many retail lenders guarantee their dollar fees now. These include

- Eloan.com,
- Indymac.com,
- HomeLoanCenter.com,
- Mortgage.com,
- Mortgage.etrade.com, and
- Countrywide.com.

If they can do it, any lender can—and they will if shoppers demand it.

Lender-controlled fees are paid to third parties for services ordered by the lender. These include the costs of appraisals, credit reports, and (when needed) pest inspections. Lenders know the prices of these services and can easily guarantee them in addition to their own fees. Countrywide.com, Mortgage.com, and Mortgage.etrade.com include appraisals and credit reports in their guarantees.

Other fees paid to third parties are not controlled by the lender, who may not know them. The most important of these are title-related services and settlement services. If you are in an area in which it can pay to shop for them, you can do it after selecting the lender. Mortgage.com includes third-party fees in its guarantee, except for charges of governments.

Other settlement costs are a miscellany of charges, which require little vigilance by the borrower.

- *Government charges*, such as transaction taxes, are costs that vary from location to location.
- *Per diem interest* is interest for the period between the closing date and the first day of the following month. At worst, the lender might try to tack on an extra day or two.
- *Escrow reserve* is your money placed on deposit with the lender so the lender can pay your taxes and insurance. The amount is based on a Department of Housing and Urban Development (HUD) formula.
- *Hazard insurance* is your homeowner's policy, which you purchase from a carrier of your choice.

In sum, in shopping lenders, you want to compare the total of *points* (including the origination fee, if any), *dollar fees*, and *lender-controlled fees* paid to third parties. Ask if they will guarantee all fees except points in writing.

The common mistake that shoppers make is to select a lender without knowing any of the lender charges except points and then try to negotiate other charges afterwards. Typically they do this after they receive a *good faith estimate* (GFE), which itemizes all the settlement costs including all lender charges.

But challenging individual cost items is not an effective way to control lender fees. The typical borrower has little to no factual basis for challenging a cost item. Even if borrowers have such knowledge, their bargaining power is weak. Having already selected the lender, few are prepared to walk from the deal—and the lender knows this.

Furthermore, even if a determined borrower succeeds in bludgeoning the lender into making a change, the determined lender can get it back somewhere else. The costs shown on the GFE are "estimates" and can be different at closing than they were the day before closing. This is a game the borrower can't win.

Some shoppers adopt a different strategy, which seems to make a lot of sense. They reason that what matters is total settlement costs, so they select the lender on that basis. Instead of shopping lender fees, they shop total settlement costs.

Indeed, this approach is the foundation of new rules regarding settlement costs that HUD has proposed and that could well be enacted in 2003. Under these rules, borrowers will be able to obtain one binding price covering all settlement costs from lenders electing this option.

Until that happens, however, borrowers can't use this strategy effectively. Lenders will not commit to any figures on total settlement costs that they might quote to shoppers. The reason is that today lenders have complete knowledge and control only over their own charges. They don't control and don't necessarily know all third-party charges, which is why the GFE is an "estimate."

Suppose, for example, you are deciding between 7% 30-year fixed-rate mortgages offered by two lenders. Lender A quotes total settlement costs of $4,000 and lender B quotes $4,200. Lender A looks like the better deal.

Closer inspection reveals, however, that A's own fees are $2,000 and A has estimated other costs of $2,000. B's own fees, in contrast, are $1,900 and B has estimated other costs at $2,300. The correct choice is B because B has the lower lender fees, which lenders can guarantee. The other costs are estimates. While we don't know which is closer to the mark, we do know that the actual figure will almost certainly not be affected by whether the shopper selects A or B.

Since lenders being shopped for total settlement costs have an incentive to err on the low side, we can guess that B's estimate probably will be closer to the mark. Whether A deliberately low-balled to get the business or made a "good faith" mistake, there is no way to know.

The bottom line is that, until HUD changes the rules, shoppers who want to control their settlement costs should focus on lender fees only.

If the shopper is dealing with a mortgage broker rather than a lender, the process is both more complicated and simpler. It is more complicated in the sense that there is one more significant fee to consider: the broker's. It is simpler in the sense that the broker keeps the lender honest on fixed-dollar fees.

While some retail lenders view fixed-dollar fees as an easy way to generate additional revenue from unwary borrowers, wholesale lenders don't because it would cause problems for their brokers. For this reason, lender fees differ very little from one wholesale lender to another. Dealing with a mortgage broker pretty much eliminates fixed-dollar lender fees as an issue to the shopper. Mortgage brokers can also help borrowers find third-party services at competitive prices.

The upshot is that shoppers who deal with a mortgage broker can shift their focus from shopping settlement costs to negotiating with the broker. Later, I will urge readers to approach the broker as a service provider who gets paid a fee that is negotiated at the outset. This is in contrast to the usual procedure of adding the broker's fee to the points charged by the lender.

Just make sure that the broker fee includes any payment to the broker from the lender. For example, if you agree on a fee of $3,000 and the broker gets $1,500 from the lender, your payment should be the difference of $1,500. Upfront Mortgage Brokers operate this way as a matter of course, but many other brokers are willing to do business this way with educated borrowers who understand the value of broker services.

32. What should I know about comparing lenders on the Web?

Comparing lenders on the Web is difficult. I have tried to help by evaluating a number of the better sites against various criteria, publishing the results at www.mtgprofessor.com. However, it takes a determined and fairly sophisticated shopper to use this type of information effectively. It is not what most shoppers want. (See the next question—"What is an upfront mortgage lender?"—for a solution to this problem.)

33. What is an "upfront mortgage lender"?

Most mortgage shoppers want a list of lenders in whom they can have confidence, who will provide them with the information they need to make an informed decision *before* applying for a mortgage, and who also guarantee them fair treatment during the period *after* they apply through to closing. To meet this need, I developed the "upfront mortgage lender" (UML) certification program. Lenders who comply with the requirements of the program are listed at www.mtgprofessor.com.

Here are the UML requirements and how they meet the needs of shoppers.

Requirement 1: A UML provides quick access to the market niches it prices on-line. The home loan market in the U.S. is divided into millions of market niches and no one lender serves them all.

Shoppers need a quick way to determine whether a particular lender prices the niche in which that shopper falls. If not, the shopper can go elsewhere without wasting time.

If the shopper's niche *is* priced on-line:

- The shopper can make valid comparisons of one UML's prices against those of another, prior to paying any fees and prior to filling out an application.
- After selecting the lender and applying for a loan, the applicant is not exposed to a future price change based on information that the lender claims not to have had at the time of the original quote.
- The applicant who elects to move to a different niche, say to a 15-year from a 30, or to pay more points to reduce the rate can check on-line to ensure that the new niche has been correctly priced.
- The applicant who elects to float rather than lock can monitor the price as it is reset daily with the market and therefore will not be overcharged on the lock day.

UMLs comply with this requirement by filling out a table on their Web site called Market Niches Priced on Line. The table format is the same at every UML, making it easy for a shopper to tell at a glance whether the lender is pricing the shopper's niche.

Requirement 2: A UML includes its fixed-dollar fees, including credit and appraisal charges, in its price and guarantees them to closing. This ensures borrowers that new fees won't be added and existing ones won't be increased after they have committed to working with the selected lender.

Requirement 3: A UML provides a clear explanation of its lock requirements. Mortgage shoppers need to know when they have the discretion to lock. The explanation should include any required payments, processes that must be completed, how expired locks are handled, and whether the borrower is committed as well as the UML.

Requirement 4: A UML discloses all the information about its ARMs needed by shoppers to make intelligent decisions. It is very difficult today to obtain the information about ARMs that is needed to make an informed decision. Loan officers selling ARMs stress one or another feature, usually the index, and leave the remainder of the ARM's features in the dark. Shoppers need information on potential ARM performance—what will happen to the interest rate and mortgage payment under assumptions about future interest rates that make sense to the shopper.

UMLs can comply with this rule in two ways. One way is to offer schedules of monthly payment and interest rate under no-change and worst-case scenarios. The first assumes that the most recent value of the index remains unchanged through the life of the loan, while the second assumes that the ARM rate increases by the maximum amount allowed in the contract.

The alternative is to provide the information needed for the shopper to calculate these (and perhaps other) scenarios using calculators at www.mtgprofessor.com or other sites. The required information will be shown on a form that will be identical for all UMLs.

Requirement 5: A UML informs borrowers if its loan officers are compensated in a way that gives them a financial incentive to overcharge the borrower. Off the Internet, many lenders credit loan officers with overages. An overage is a price higher than the price delivered to the loan officer by the lender's pricing department. For example, if the price shown on the loan officer's price sheet is 6% at zero points and the loan officer sells the deal for 6% and 1 point (an upfront charge equal to 1% of the loan), there is an overage of 1 point. If the loan officer gets a piece of it, there is a conflict situation that the customer ought to know about.

34. What is an "upfront mortgage broker"?

An "upfront mortgage broker" (UMB) is one who has elected to do business in an up-front and fully transparent way. For a list of official UMBs, see www.mtgprofessor.com. Here are the major differences between a UMB and a conventional mortgage broker (MB):

1. *UMBs disclose their fees to customers in advance and in writing, and disclose the* wholesale *prices (rates and points) passed through from lenders.* Customers of UMBs pay the broker's fee plus wholesale loan prices. In contrast, conventional MBs add a markup to the wholesale prices and quote the resulting "retail prices" to customers. Most MBs reveal their markup only in required disclosures after an application has been submitted.
2. *The UMBs' interests are fully aligned with those of customers.* They can thus represent borrowers in shopping for loans. In contrast, MBs shopping the market are often in a conflict situation with customers. For example:
   - The loan type that best meets the customer's needs may not be the one that allows the largest markup for the MB.
   - MBs may profit by ignoring customer requests to lock the rate/points, putting the customer at risk.
   - MBs often increase their markup on customers who allow the rate/points to float, by not giving them the best available rate (the float rate) when the loan is finally locked.
3. *UMBs credit customers with any rebates they receive from third parties.* Mortgage brokers sometimes receive rebates from lenders or concessions from home sellers. UMBs credit customers for any such payments that would otherwise increase the

broker's fee beyond what was agreed upon. In contrast, MBs may or may not credit customers for payments from third parties, depending on the circumstances.

35. Who is most likely to refer me to a good lender?

A borrower can always depend on luck, by throwing a dart at the yellow pages. A referral is of value if it raises the probability of a good outcome above that from throwing the dart. The four major sources of referrals are real estate sales agents, other borrowers, Internet referral sites, and builders.

Home purchasers accept more referrals from real estate sales agents than from all other sources combined. Sales agent referrals generally are to individual loan officers or brokers, as opposed to firms. An agent with great confidence in a loan officer will continue to refer clients even when the loan officer switches firms.

Sales agents have the same interest as buyers in completing transactions. Hence, they refer clients to loan providers who can generally be depended upon to close on time. This is the agent's major concern, and it is a concern of borrowers as well.

Sales agents have no comparable interest in the mortgage price or whether the borrower is placed in the right kind of mortgage. However, the agent doesn't want the price to be so far out of line or the service so abysmal that the borrower throws a fit and blames the agent. Hence, referrals from sales agents are significantly better than throwing a dart at the yellow pages.

Referrals from other borrowers are usually based on a single transaction. They are better than the yellow pages, but not much better. I have seen borrowers who were very pleased with their experience because they were not aware that they had seriously overpaid. I have also seen the reverse—borrowers who bad-mouthed their loan provider, who had done the best possible job under adverse circumstances and had earned very little on the deal. Before acting on a borrower referral, grill the borrower about the basis for his or her opinion.

Internet referral sites provide price information for a large number of lenders and mortgage brokers, usually listed by state. They also provide quick entree to the Web sites of each loan provider listed. In theory, a borrower can sort through the list of loan providers, identify those with the lowest prices, and visit the individual Web sites to make a final selection.

To check on whether that strategy would work, I examined six referral sites:

- Bankrate.com
- BestRate.com
- CompareInterestRates.com
- Domania.com
- Interest.com
- LoanPage.com

I found that, in many cases, the lenders quoting the best prices on the referral sites were either quoting higher prices on their own sites or not providing complete price information on their own sites. I concluded that referral sites were no better than the yellow pages.

36. What's the difference between a mortgage broker and a lender—and what's the advantage of using a broker?

A mortgage broker offers the loan products of different lenders, but does not lend. A lender makes the final decision regarding loan approval and provides the money to the borrower at the closing table.

Mortgage brokers counsel borrowers on any problems involved in qualifying for a loan, including credit problems. Brokers also help borrowers select the loan that best meet their needs and shop for the best deal among the lenders offering that type of loan.

Brokers take applications from borrowers and lock the rate and other terms with lenders. They also provide borrowers with the many disclosures required by the federal and state governments.

In addition, brokers compile all the documents required for transactions, including the credit report, property appraisal, verification of employment and assets, and so on. Not until a file is complete is it handed off to the lender, who approves and funds the loan.

The main advantage mortgage brokers have over lenders is their access to loan programs from many lenders. The mortgage market is complex and subdivided into countless niches and no one lender offers loans in every niche. For example, many lenders won't offer loans to borrowers with poor credit, borrowers who can't document their income, borrowers who can't make any down payment, borrowers who want to purchase a condominium as an investment, borrowers with very high debts, borrowers who need to close within 72 hours, or borrowers who reside abroad. The list goes on and on. But there are lenders in every one of these niches and brokers can find them.

Brokers are also experts at shopping the market. They receive price updates every day on all major programs from all the lenders they deal with. Price differences from lender to lender in the wholesale market in which they operate are much smaller than comparable differences in the retail market. Whether the broker uses that shopping ability to benefit the borrower or himself or herself is another question.

37. How do mortgage brokers make money?

The lenders that mortgage brokers deal with quote *wholesale* prices, leaving it to the brokers to add a markup. The wholesale price plus the markup equals the *retail* price the broker quotes to the consumer.

For example, one wholesale price on a particular

program might be 7% and 0 points, to which the broker adds a markup of 2 points, resulting in a retail price to the customer of 7% and 2 points. In this case, the borrower pays the 2 points. Another wholesale price on the same program might be 7.25% plus a 1.5-point rebate (negative points), which when marked up would be 7.25% plus .5 points. In this case, the borrower pays the broker .5 points and the lender pays the broker 1.5 points.

38. Won't I pay less if I go directly to the broker?

You could pay less, or you could pay more. The wholesale prices that lenders quote to brokers are lower than the retail prices lenders quote to borrowers because of the work that brokers do for them that lenders would otherwise have to do themselves. In addition to getting a wholesale price, borrowers benefit from the brokers' superior ability to shop the market. If the wholesale-retail price spread plus the savings from better shopping exceed the broker's fee, you pay less dealing with a broker.

39. What are the disadvantages of using a mortgage broker?

A lender will honor a mistake in the customer's favor made by one of its employees, but probably won't honor a mistake made by a mortgage broker. In addition, some borrowers find comfort in dealing with a large lender with a recognizable name. Brokers are not known nationally, although they may be well known locally, especially by the real estate agents from whom they receive referrals.

40. Are brokers more likely to take advantage of me than lenders?

That is not at all clear. There are predators in both groups, but there are no data on how they break down as between brokers and lenders. It would be unwise to assume that because you are dealing with a lender, you are safe.

41. How can I be sure I'm not being taken advantage of?

Find a mortgage broker who is willing to work as your agent at a fee agreed upon in advance. The fee includes your payment and any compensation the broker receives from the lender. The broker passes through the wholesale prices, which are disclosed to you, without any markup.

Upfront mortgage brokers, listed at www.mtgprofessor.com, prefer to work in this way. But many other brokers would be willing to if customers requested it. To avoid misunderstandings or surprises, the broker's compensation should be stipulated at the outset, in writing, signed by the broker and by you. The document should state:

> The total compensation to [name of broker], including any rebates from the lender, will be _____________. A separate processing fee will be ____________.

42. What is the downside of using a brand-name lender?

Many borrowers go to lenders whose name they recognize because, in a complex market filled with booby traps and predators, name recognition provides comfort. The logic of this approach is that a lender with a reputation to protect is not going to jeopardize it by exploiting borrowers.

On the other hand, name lenders tend to price a little above the market. They like to say that they provide better service than bargain-basement lenders. What they mean is that borrowers should be willing to pay something more for the comfort of dealing with them.

How much more is difficult to say. It varies across products and it also depends on how well you deal with the loan officer. While the lender may be known worldwide, you must negotiate your deal with loan officer Joe Smith, who operates on commission and has some discretion in pricing loans. If Joe tabs you as unknowledgeable and timid, you may well pay an "overage"—a price above the price listed on the loan officer's price sheet. The lender and the loan officer usually share overages. On the other hand, if you are smart and forceful, you might negotiate an underage—a price below the listed price. This could be as good a deal as you might get anywhere else. But there are many more overages than underages.

The bottom line is that you may pay a premium price dealing with a name lender, especially if you pay an overage. But name lenders cap the size of overages, so the overpayment won't be outrageous.

43. What should I know about mortgage auction sites like Lendingtree.com?

Mortgage auction sites such as LendingTree.com pull together a group of up to four lenders who bid for your loan. I once called them "lead-generation sites," because from a lender's perspective, that is what they do. A "lead" is a packet of information about a consumer in the market for a loan. Lenders pay for leads and auction sites are an important source of them.

I recently looked at nine mortgage auction sites: Cityloans.com, GetSmart.com, InterestRatesOnline.com, LendingTree.com, LoanApp.com, LoanHounds.com, LoanWeb.com, LowestMortgage.com, and MortgageExpo.com. While LendingTree is ahead of the others, their similarities are more important than their differences.

All of these sites essentially work the same way. The prospective borrower fills out a questionnaire covering the loan request, property, personal finances, and contact information. The sites use this information to select the lenders to whom the information is sent. Lenders then prepare an offer to the borrower based on the same information.

The sites send the information provided by applicants to "up to four" lenders, except for MortgageExpo.com, which sends it to only one. Lenders are selected based on prior information provided by the lenders regarding the types of loans, borrowers, and properties that they are prepared to consider. For example, an applicant with poor credit who wants to purchase a condominium would not be referred to a lender who has told the site it only wants loans to A-quality borrowers purchasing or refinancing single-family homes. Similarly, an applicant who doesn't want to document income or assets would not be sent to a lender who always requires full documentation.

In principle, the lender selection function performed by auction sites should be particularly valuable to borrowers with one or more challenging features, such as poor credit, incomplete documentation, or little cash. Such borrowers can avoid wasting time soliciting lenders who won't deal with them. How well the sites perform this function, however, is difficult to determine.

The lender-screening process employed by the auction sites also provides some protection against falling into the hands of rogues—lenders or mortgage brokers out to extract as much revenue as possible from every customer. The sites have every reason to bounce a lender who attracts multiple complaints from borrowers. Only LendingTree.com, however, has developed a rating system for its lenders based on reports from borrowers.

In sum, auction sites may be useful in screening out rogues and allowing borrowers with poor credit, incomplete documentation, or little cash to find lenders that deal in those market niches. Such borrowers will probably do better at auction sites than by throwing darts against the yellow pages or visiting single-lender sites. (With few exceptions, single-lender sites don't quote prices that apply to those borrowers.) Strong borrowers who can find their desired loans priced on single-lender sites will probably do better shopping those.

Here are some suggestions for using an auction site effectively:

- Before using the site, decide whether you want a fixed- or adjustable-rate mortgage, as well as your preferred loan term, down payment, and points. Auctions can't work if the item being sold is not precisely defined. If necessary, do some homework. If you would rather not bother, see a mortgage broker.
- Fill out the questionnaire as accurately and completely as you can. The information you provide is used with information the site has on the preferences of its lenders to match you with the lenders most likely to be interested in your loan.
- Mortgage price information comes not from the site but from the lenders who contact you. The amount of price information they give you may depend on what you ask for. On fixed-rate mortgages, you need the interest rate, points, and dollar fees. While some lenders are not in the habit of providing their dollar fees in initial price quotes, you should insist upon it. On adjustable-rate mortgages, you need to know more than the rate, points, and loan fees; also ask the lenders for the interest rate index, margin, all rate adjustment caps, and maximum rate. With that information, you can use calculators 7b and 7c at www.mtgprofessor.com to see how the payment might change.
- Receiving price quotes over the telephone is looking for trouble because you have nothing in writing. Ask lenders to e-mail or fax their prices to you.

- The interest rate and points quoted to you by a lender apply only on the day you receive them. The lender is not bound to them the following day, since the market may have changed. For the same reason, it is not safe to compare a price received on Monday from one lender with a price received on Tuesday from another.
- The prices that really matter are those quoted to you on the day you lock the loan with the lender. The lock means that the lender is committed to the prices.
- Since locking imposes costs on lenders, they want some evidence of your commitment to the deal before they will lock. Their requirements vary widely, however, ranging from very little to a signed application to a signed application plus a nonrefundable payment. You are entitled to know at the outset exactly what each lender's requirements are and how long it should take if you do everything expected of you. Ask!
- Since you selected the lender based on the initial price quote but it is the locked price that you are going to pay, you have a right to know how the lender will set the price on the day you lock. You need not accept a statement that the new price "will be at the market." The answer you are looking for is that the lock price will be the same as the price the lender is quoting to new customers on the identical loan on the same day. Ask if the lender has a Web site that contains up-to-date prices that you can use to monitor your price day by day. If it does not, ask the loan officer how he or she intends to demonstrate that you have received the correct price.
- Unlike rates and points, loan fees are not market-driven. Unless you change one or more of the loan characteristics, there is seldom a good reason for these fees to change between the time

you receive the initial price quote and the time you close. Some lenders will guarantee these fees in writing if you ask. They may even be willing to include appraisal fees and credit charges in the guarantee, because they order them and know how much they cost.

44. Should I respond to solicitations?

Usually, it is a bad idea. Your chances of selecting a predator are higher if you respond to a solicitation than if you throw a dart at the yellow pages. Not all lenders who solicit are predators, but all predators solicit.

In general, the more costly the mode of solicitation, the greater the likelihood that the soliciting loan provider is a predator. E-mail solicitations are the least costly and the least indicative of predatory intent. In contrast, the solicitor who knocks on your back door, selling home improvements along with the loan, is very likely to be a predator.

Lenders who solicit their own customers to refinance are an exception to the generalization. On the other hand, it is foolish to accept an offer to refinance from your current lender without checking the offer against other loan sources. The customers that lenders select to solicit are those who the lenders fear may refinance elsewhere. The deals they offer, however, while better than those borrowers have now, may well be inferior to those available from other sources.

Chapter 7

Locking the Interest Rate

45. When should you lock in an interest rate?

Locking the loan protects the borrower against the possibility of an increase in market interest rates during the period between the lock date and the loan closing.

A lock commits the lender to lend at a specified interest rate and points, provided the loan is closed within the specified "lock period." For example, a lender agrees to lock a 30-year fixed-rate mortgage of $200,000 at 7.5% and 1 point for 30 days. The lock lapses if the loan does not close within 30 days.

A lock imposes a cost on the lender, and the longer the lock period, the higher the cost. This cost is embedded in the price quoted to borrowers. The lender who quotes 7.5% and 1 point for a 30-day lock, for example, might charge .875 points for a 15-day lock, and 1.125-1.25 points for a 60-day lock.

Some borrowers elect to "float" the rate, meaning not to lock it, as long as possible. If the market is stable, they expect to benefit from the declining lock price. They may also believe that market rates will decline.

It would be foolhardy for home purchasers who barely qualify at today's rates, to take the risk of a rate increase. But even if qualification is not an issue, floating past the point where you can change loan providers is hazardous if you have no way to monitor the market price on the day you finally lock. If the market price on the day you lock is what the loan provider says it is, you are at his mercy. Some will pad the price just because you have nowhere to go. On a refinance, you can always change loan providers, so it's safer to delay the lock until shortly before closing.

Allowing the price to float on a purchase transaction is safe if you have a way to check the market price on the day you lock. If you originally shopped the lender's Web site and found your price there, you can check it again on the lock day. Alternatively, you can deal with an upfront mortgage broker who charges a set fee above the wholesale price, and who will reveal the wholesale price on the lock day. Otherwise, don't float.

46. When should you let your interest rate float?

Borrowers who are refinancing can monitor the floating interest rate/points quoted to them by the broker against other market information, and if the quote appears out of line they can bail out. Home purchasers with a scheduled closing, however, inevitably reach a point of no return where it is too late to begin the mortgage shopping process anew. During a refinance boom, when loan processing takes longer, the point of no return might be 45 days rather than the 30 days that might suffice in a more normal market.

To protect themselves, I recommend that borrowers not float past the point where they can bail out and shop elsewhere. Alternatively, they should pin down the lender or broker on an objective procedure for determining the market interest rate. One simple and fair rule is that the market rate will be the rate that the lender is quoting to potential new customers on the same day. If you lock only a few days before closing, your rate should be the lender's current float rate. If you lock 15 days before closing, your rate should be the lender's 15-day lock rate on that day. And so on.

One advantage of dealing with a lender or broker who quotes prices on the Internet is that they provide you with the data you need to monitor the rate they give you when you lock.

47. What happens if the lock expires before the loan closes?

The policy of most lenders is to extend the lock at the same terms if market rates have declined or stayed the same. If rates have risen, however, they will usually only extend at the higher market rate. Lenders may make an occasional exception if they are solely to blame for delays that cause the lock expiration, but don't count on it. Sorting out responsibility is extremely difficult.

Lock expirations are common during a refinance boom when lenders, mortgage brokers, appraisers and escrow agents are swamped with more work than they can handle, and many deals don't get done on time. During such periods, lenders generally give purchasers a priority. Delayed refinancings can be rescheduled, but not completing a purchase mortgage on time can jeopardize the purchase, at high cost to buyers. It could also jeopardize lenders' relationships with real estate brokers, upon whom many depend for borrower referrals.

To minimize the possibility that your lock will expire before you close, select the lock period only after you have asked the loan provider how long the lender's turn-around time is. During a refinance boom, add 15 days to it. In addition, get all your documents available so they can be produced when needed. Be available to answer questions or provide additional documents during the entire period the loan is in process.

If you are using a mortgage broker, interview this person about his or her workload. The broker should be an expediter but too often he or she becomes a drag. Deals from harassed brokers who submit incomplete and inaccurate files are likely to languish in the lender's pile of incomplete applications.

48. Is locking with a mortgage broker the same as locking with a lender?

Not quite. In most cases, the broker will follow your instructions, locking with the lender when you tell him to. Some brokers, however, will charge borrowers the lock price but won't lock with the lender. If the market doesn't change, they pocket the price difference.

Brokers rationalize this practice on the grounds that they protect the borrower themselves. The broker absorbs the loss if interest rates go against them. But it is fair-weather protection that disappears when the consumer needs it most—during an interest rate spike.

For example, in the two-month period January-March 1980, rates on 30-year fixed-rate mortgages jumped from 12.88% to 15.28%. A broker who locked for 60 days at 12.88% would have to pay a lender about 15 points to accept a loan with that rate in a 15.28% market. The broker would either go out of business, or deny that a lock was given. (Broker locks are oral commitments.) The borrower would be left high and dry in either case.

Broker locks are a deceitful practice because the borrower is led to believe that the lender is providing the lock. To protect yourself, insist on receiving the rate lock commitment letter from the lender identifying you as the applicant.

49. Does a lock commit the borrower as well as the lender?

In principal, it does. A borrower who wants to be protected against a rate increase during the lock period, but would like to take advantage of a rate decline, can purchase a "float-down." A float-down provides the same upside protection as a lock, plus an option to reduce the rate if market rates decline. Since it carries more value to the borrower than a lock, and is more costly to the lender to provide, the borrower pays more for it. A lender who charges 1.25 points for a 60-day lock might charge 1.75 points for a 60-day float-down.

Many refinancing borrowers pay for a lock but act as if they have a float-down. If rates decline during the lock period, they demand a lower rate and if they don't get it, they start anew with another loan provider. I call them "lock-jumpers."

I once criticized lock-jumpers, going so far as to compare them to shoplifters. But the following letter caused me to reconsider.

"Why would a 'lock-jumper' be considered a shoplifter? It seems to me that most lenders and brokers don't tell the borrower that a lock is binding on them if rates go down, and generally the borrower doesn't sign anything indicating such a commitment. If they had wanted a commitment, they should have asked for one."

This reader makes a very good point. If a broker or lender allows ambiguity regarding the borrower's commitment under a rate lock, then the borrower is entitled to interpret that ambiguity as he or she pleases. Lock-jumping is OK, in other words, unless the borrower has committed him or herself in writing not to do it.

Chapter 8

Refinancing Your Mortgage

50. When does refinancing really pay?

To save money, you must stay in your house longer than the "break-even period"—the period over which the interest savings just cover the refinance costs. The larger the spread between the new interest rate and the rate on your existing loan, the shorter the break-even period. The more it costs to obtain the new loan, the longer the break-even period.

But beware! *The break-even period is not the cost of the new loan divided by the reduction in the monthly mortgage payment.* This widely used rule of thumb is a misapplication of the principle that when explaining something to the consumer one should "keep it simple." Simple is good, except when it's wrong!

Among other things, the rule of thumb does not allow for the difference in how rapidly you pay off the new loan as opposed to the old one. Let's say that in 1992 you took out an 11% 30-year fixed rate loan, which now has a $100,000 balance and 21 years to run. You refinance into a 7% 15-year loan at a cost of $3,750.

- Monthly payment on the old loan = $1019
- Monthly payment on the new loan = $899
- Reduction in monthly payment = $120
- $3750 divided by $120 = 31 months

The rule of thumb says that you break-even in 31

months. However, because of the shorter term and lower rate on the new loan, in 31 months you would owe $7,041 less than you would have owed on the old loan. So, the rule of thumb in this case seriously overstates the break-even period. Taking account of differences in the loan balance, you would actually be ahead of the game in 12 months, as shown below:

- Savings in monthly payment: $120 for 12 months = $1440
- Plus lower loan balance in month 12: $2620
- Equals total saving from refinance: $4060
- Less refinance cost: $3750
- Equals net gain: $310

Next consider the case where an 11% loan taken out in 1992 was for 15 years, and now has only 6 years to run, while you plan to refinance into a 30-year loan. With the remaining term shorter on the old loan and longer on the new one, the difference in monthly payment rises to $1238. Using the rule of thumb the $3750 cost would be recovered in only 3 months. But this fails to consider the slower loan repayment on the new loan. Taking account of the slower repayment, you don't actually come out ahead until 14 months out.

The rule of thumb (dividing the upfront cost by the reduction in mortgage payment) approximates the true break-even period only if the term on your new loan is close to the unexpired term on your old loan. In other circumstances it can lead you seriously astray.

The rule of thumb also ignores other factors that affect the break-even period. These include the time value of money, taxes, and differences in the cost of mortgage insurance between the old and new mortgage. (Read "What should enter the refinance decision?")

51. What should enter the refinance decision?

If the purpose of the refinance is to reduce costs, as

opposed to raising cash, you should refinance if your total costs are lower with the new mortgage than with your current mortgage, over the period you expect to have the new mortgage.

This approach is used in calculator 3a at www.mtg-professor.com. It shows all the costs over a specified period of an existing and a new mortgage side by side. It also shows the "break-even period," which is the *minimum* length of time the borrower must hold the new mortgage to make the refinancing pay. So even if you are not sure how long you will have the mortgage, if you are confident that you will have it longer than the break-even period, you know the refinance pays.

I will illustrate with the case of Jane who had a $320,000 loan balance at 6.25% with 25 years to go. Her potential new loan was at 5.25% for 30 years, with cash payments of 2 points (2% of the loan balance, or $6400) plus $2200 for other settlement costs. She guessed she would keep the new mortgage 5 years.

The calculator divided her costs into three groups:

1. *Upfront costs* consisting of points and settlement costs, were $8600 on the new loan, zero on the old one.
2. *Monthly payments of principal and interest* were $106,024 on the new loan and $126,657 on the old one. (These numbers are calculated by multiplying the monthly payments by 60).
3. *Lost interest* was $7057 on the new loan, $7216 on the old one.

The last item is the interest Jane would have earned on upfront and monthly payments if she had saved those monies at 2.24%, her after-tax savings rate. Loan officers sometimes claim that borrowers don't understand lost interest. My experience is that most borrowers do understand that money they spend could have earned interest if they hadn't spent it. Lost interest, however, can easily be excluded from the analysis by setting the savings rate to zero.

The calculator factors in two cost offsets:

- *Tax savings on interest and points* was $23,469 on the new loan, $25,753 on the old one. Jane's tax rate of 25.5% was used in this calculation.
- *Reduction in loan balance* was $25,122 on the new loan, $31,198 on the old one. In both cases, these were measured from the original balance of $320,000.

Deducting the cost offsets from the costs, Jane's new mortgage had a net cost of $73,089 as compared to $76,922 for the old one. Refinancing would thus save her $3833 over the 5 years. The calculator also indicated that her break-even period was 39 months.

The fact that this refinancing made Jane better off doesn't mean it was the best. For example, Jane could have replaced the 30-year 5.25% loan with one for 15 years at 5%. Assuming everything else was the same, this shift to a 15-year would increase the net gain from refinancing from $3833 to $6098, while reducing the break-even period from 39 to 35 months.

Many borrowers who refinance today finance the upfront costs. They add the costs to the mortgage rather than pay them in cash. Calculator 3a at www.mtgprofessor.com allows the user to select the financing option.

Those who try the option find that it reduces the gains from refinancing. This is largely because the borrower must pay interest on the costs at the mortgage rate. If Jane had financed the upfront costs of her new 30-year loan, the net gain from the refinance would have dropped from $3833 to $1240, while the break-even period would have increased from 39 to 53 months.

Financing the costs, furthermore, can flip the loan amount above 80% of the property value, which triggers mortgage insurance. If the borrower is already paying mortgage insurance, it can raise the premium.

If this had happened with Jane's 30-year loan, the small gain from refinancing would have become a loss. Fortunately, she had enough equity to avoid mortgage insurance altogether. The calculator automatically factors mortgage insurance into the cost calculation, if it arises.

A side benefit from using a calculator is that it forces borrowers to collect all the information that affects the profitability of a refinance. Once all the relevant information is at hand, it is clear that no two cases are exactly alike. Fortunately, the calculator will handle them all.

52. Should I consolidate credit card debt in a second mortgage?

The argument for consolidation is that it will reduce interest costs. The interest rate on a second mortgage is usually well below rates on credit cards, and mortgage interest is also tax deductible. The savings can be substantial.

Consolidation, however, has important disadvantages that should be carefully weighed in making a decision. Perhaps the most important, at least for some borrowers, is that consolidation converts unsecured debt to debt secured by your home. If a financial reversal in the future makes it impossible to service credit card debt, you can stop paying. You will lose your good credit rating, but if you can continue to service your first mortgage, you won't lose your home.

Another disadvantage of consolidation it that the new second mortgage may hamper your ability to refinance the first mortgage if a profitable opportunity to do so appears. When a first mortgage is paid off, an existing second mortgage automatically becomes a first mortgage. This makes it impossible to replace the old first mortgage with a new one unless the second mortgage lender provides the refinancing lender with a written statement indicating a willingness to subordinate the second mortgage to a new first mortgage. Many second mortgage lenders will do this, charging fees that range from nominal to extortionate, but some won't do it at all.

If you are paying for mortgage insurance on your first mortgage, adding a second mortgage will probably extend the period over which you must pay. Under prevailing rules for terminating mortgage insurance, the balance of the first mortgage must be paid down to a lower level if there is a second mortgage (see "How do I cancel private mortgage insurance?").

If the second mortgage results in your total mortgage debt exceeding the value of the property, you may lose your mobility. Suppose you are offered a better job in another city that would require that you relocate. If you owe $120,000 on a $100,000 house, selling the house means finding $20,000 in cash to pay off both mortgages. If you can't find the cash, the only way to relocate is to default, which would prevent you from buying a house in your new location. I have received a number of letters from people who have found themselves in exactly this situation, asking whether they can transfer the second mortgage to a new house! Of course, they can't.

Finally, consolidation that results in lower monthly payments can tempt short-sighted borrowers into building up their credit card balances all over again. This is why I advise borrowers who are not dissuaded by the arguments against consolidation, to avoid a large drop in the monthly payment. Shift the second mortgage to 10 or 15 years, whichever provides a total payment close to the one you have now. With the lower rate and short term, you will at least have a fighting chance of becoming an equity-builder rather than a credit card junky.

53. Does it ever make sense to refinance at a higher rate?

Borrowers refinance for three reasons: to raise cash, to reduce monthly payments, or to lower interest costs.

Refinancing at a higher interest rate in order to raise cash, or to lower monthly payments, may be justified but often isn't, for reasons explained below. Refinancing at a higher interest rate in order to lower interest costs is *never* justified, although there are some snake oil salesmen in the market who would like to convince you otherwise. I'll explain their tricks further below.

Raising Cash: Refinancing to raise cash means that you borrow more than the balance of the old mortgage. This is called a "cash-out refinance." Very often, the rate on a cash-out refinance is higher than the rate on the mortgage that is being paid off.

I can't say that this is *never* a sensible thing to do. If a family member is critically ill, and if a cash-out refinance is the only source of cash for a life-saving operation, then you do it. Yet the number of rate-increasing cash-out refinances that can be justified by dire circumstances is very small. In all too many cases, the borrower had a better option but didn't realize it.

For example, Betty had a $210,000 mortgage at 7% and needed $18,000. She took a cash-out refinance for $232,000 at 7.5%, which covered the $18,000 she needed and $4,000 of settlement costs. She could have obtained a second mortgage for $18,000 but decided against it because the rate was 10.5%. That was a mistake.

What Betty overlooked was that if she took the second mortgage, she would be paying 10.5% on only $18,000, while retaining the $210,000 loan at 7%. With the cash-out refinance, in contrast, the rate on $210,000 was raised by .5%. Paying 7.5% on $232,000 costs more than paying 7% on $210,000 and 10.5% on $18,000.

Unfortunately, the Truth in Lending (TIL) disclosures provided to Betty encouraged her to make this mistake. They indicated an Annual Percentage Rate (APR) of 7.60% on the cash-out refinance, and 10.90% on the second mortgage. Illogically, the APR on her cash-out refinance did not take into account the cost of raising the rate on $210,000 by .5%.

An APR on a cash-out refinance that is comparable to an APR on a second mortgage would be based on the net cash raised, not on the total loan amount. This "net-cash" APR was 14.82%, which was well above the 10.90% APR on the second. If the net-cash APR had been provided to Betty, she might well have avoided the mistake.

The Federal Reserve administers TIL but doesn't expect it to fix this problem anytime soon. Meanwhile, you can compare the cost of a cash-out refinance and a second mortgage using calculator 3d at www.mtgprofessor.com.

Reducing Monthly Payments: While refinancing at a higher rate to lower monthly payments is nowhere near as common as refinancing to get cash, it happens occasionally. The payment can be reduced only if the remaining term on the existing mortgage is short. This allows a lengthening of the term to reduce the payment by more than the higher rate increases it.

Charles took out a 15-year mortgage in early 1994 at 6.5%, and has paid down the balance to $200,000. But Charles' income has unexpectedly dropped and he can no longer afford the mortgage payment of $2,970. He plans to refinance into a 30-year loan at 7% on which the payment is only $1,331, but at a cost of $3,500.

At my suggestion, Charles asked his servicing agent whether it would be possible to extend the term of his existing loan, or reduce the payment to interest-only for 5 years. In cases where a servicing agent also owns the loan, the agent may be willing to do this for a small fee to accommodate a customer. However, the answer to Charles was "no," because the agent did not own the loan and had no discretion to adjust the terms.

In fact, the loan was in a pool of similar loans against which a mortgage-backed security had been issued and sold to multiple investors. Changing the terms of loans in pools against which securities have been issued is forbidden. While the "securitization" of mortgages has driven down interest rates by increasing the efficiency of the system, it has eliminated the flexibility to negotiate changes in the contract. Charles was forced to pay the $3500 in refinance fees.

Reducing Interest Costs: If the purpose is to reduce your interest costs, it *never* makes sense to refinance at a higher interest rate. To an economist, this is self-evident, yet hardly a week goes by that I don't hear from confused homeowners who are being badgered by snake oil salesmen trying to convince them that *their* higher rates actually cost less.

54. When is no-cost refinance a good deal?

If you expect to be out of your house within 2 or 3 years, or you are not sure and want to hedge, the no-cost loan can be a good deal. If your time horizon is longer, the no-cost loan should be avoided. There is no reason to choose a no-cost loan because you are strapped for cash, since it is usually possible to include the costs of refinancing in the new loan.

If you shop for a no-cost loan, make sure that you and the lender agree on exactly what it means. It is not "zero points" which leaves you responsible for other types of lender fees as well as other payments to third parties. It is not "zero fees" which still leaves you responsible for payments to third parties. And it is not "no cash" because that could mean that you are paying the costs but the lender is increasing the loan by enough to cover them. On a true "no-cost" loan, the lender collects no fees and pays all other settlement costs on your behalf without increasing the loan amount.

There are only two kinds of payments borrowers should expect to make on a true no-cost loan. One is per diem interest, which is interest from the day of closing to the first day of the following month. On a refinance, you will also pay interest from the first of the month to the closing day. The other outlay you should expect to pay is escrows, though on a refinance you will get credit for escrows held by the old lender.

I am frequently asked whether you can tell if you have a no-cost loan from the APR? The answer is "yes and no." If the APR is greater than the interest rate it means that you are paying some lender fees and don't have a no-cost loan. However, the fact that the APR equals the interest rate doesn't necessarily mean that you have a no-cost loan because not all settlement costs are included in the APR. You are not paying any of the fees that are included in the APR, but you might still be paying some other settlement costs.

My way of assessing a no-cost option is to view the costs that I would otherwise have to pay as an investment on which I can calculate a yield. Since the interest rate is significantly lower when you pay the costs yourself, the monthly mortgage payment is lower, and the balance is paid down faster. The lower payments and faster repayment of the loan balance is the return on investment.

When I have made this calculation at various times, I found that if the loan remains in force for only 12 months, my return would be negative and the no-cost loan would be the better choice. If the loan runs for 24 months the return on my investment would be 7.7%, which is a so-so return that would leave me on the cusp. If the loan runs for 36 months, however, the return would be 31%, which is a clear winner. These numbers should be typical of those you would find if you shopped the market yourself.

The upshot is that no-cost loans are a good option if you expect to move within 2 years, and a poor option if you expect to remain for 3 years or more. The longer you expect to be in the house, the more attractive it becomes to pay the settlement costs in order to get the lower interest rate.

A no-cost loan might also be a useful stopgap in situations where you think you might move shortly but aren't sure. You can save some money while waiting for the situation to clarify, and if it turns out that you are going to stay put after all, you can refinance again later.

55. Should you refinance with your current lender?

The case for refinancing with your current lender is that this lender may be in a position to waive some settlement costs because you are an existing customer. The case against is that that lender may offer a deal that is better than the one you have but inferior to one you might obtain elsewhere. Hence, I recommend shopping other lenders first, and your current lender last.

In a refinance market, lenders are conflicted with regard to how they treat their existing borrowers. They don't want to encourage any of their borrowers to refinance who might otherwise not get around to it. On the other hand, if they know that a borrower is going to refinance regardless, they want the new loan. To get it, many lenders have what are called "retention" programs, which are designed to recapture as many as possible of those borrowers who are determined to refinance, without putting any refinance ideas into the heads of other borrowers. Distinguishing the two groups is not easy, but there are ways.

For example, if you call your lender to find out the exact balance of your loan and your lender has a retention program, you will quickly receive a call from its loan origination department offering to refinance your loan. A balance inquiry usually means the borrower is looking to refinance.

The lender to whom you are now remitting your payments may be in a position to offer you lower settlement costs than a new lender, but this can vary from case to case. The greatest potential for lower settlement costs arises where the current lender was the originating lender and still owns your loan, a common situation with loans made by banks and savings and loan associations. If your payment record has been good, the lender may forgo a credit report, property appraisal, title search and other risk control procedures that are otherwise mandatory on new loans. This is strictly up to the lender.

Indeed, if you are not looking to take any cash out of the transaction and are looking only to reduce the interest rate, the lender may elect simply to reduce the interest rate on your current loan rather than refinance. This avoids all settlement costs.

If the lender to whom you are now remitting your payments is the originating lender but no longer owns the loan, the potential for lower settlement costs is less. In this case, your lender does not have the same discretion to forego settlement procedures but must follow the guidelines laid down by the owner of the loan. If the loan had earlier been sold to one of the federal secondary market agencies, Fannie Mae or Freddie Mac, the guidelines are theirs. While both agencies have provisions for "streamlined refinancing documentation," the discretion granted the lender, and therefore the potential cost savings, is quite limited.

The potential for lower settlement costs is least when the lender to whom you are now remitting your payments is neither the originating lender or the current owner. This is a fairly common situation that arises when the contract to service the loan is sold. In this case, your lender may not be in a position to use all of the streamlined refinancing procedures because its files do not contain some of the information those procedures require, such as the original appraisal report.

The greater the potential for lower settlement costs from dealing with your present lender, the more likely that that lender can offer you the best terms. Which doesn't necessarily mean that he will. The reason for going to your present lender last is to make sure that you receive the benefit of any cost reductions.

56. Why must I buy a new title insurance policy when I refinance?

Because the lender's policy terminates when the loan is paid off. Furthermore, the lender wants protection against title issues that may have arisen since you purchased the property, such as the lien mentioned previously. A new title search will uncover the lien, and you will have to pay it off as a condition for the refinance.

The good news is that insurers generally offer discounts on policies taken out within short periods after the preceding policy. In some cases, discounts are available as far out as 6 years from the date of the previous policy. But you may not get the discount if you don't ask.

Chapter 9

After the Loan Has Closed

57. Is paying down my loan early a good investment?

The repayment of principal on a mortgage is an investment that yields a return equal to the interest rate on the mortgage.

Suppose, for example, you add $100 to the scheduled mortgage payment. This makes the loan balance at the end of the month $100 less than it would have been without the extra payment. In the months that follow, you save the interest on that $100 that you otherwise would have paid. Since the interest payment that you would have made is determined by the interest rate on your mortgage, the yield on your $100 investment is equal to that rate. A prepayment penalty, however, would reduce the yield.

To determine whether paying more principal is a good investment, the interest rate should be compared to the yield on alternative investments having minimal risk. There is zero risk on loan repayment.

If the mortgage rate is 8% and the alternative yield is a 4% bank deposit, for example, your future wealth will be greater if you use your excess income to repay principal rather than putting it in the bank. After any period, the reduction in the loan balance would be greater than the increase in the bank account.

58. What should you do when you can't pay your mortgage?

People who suffer financial reverses may find themselves in a situation where they know they can't continue making their mortgage payments. If this happens, you should develop a game plan *before* you become delinquent. Here are the major components of such a plan.

Document your loss of income. This will position you to demonstrate to the lender that your inability to pay is involuntary, should this be necessary later on.

Estimate your equity in the house. Your equity is what you could sell it for net of sales commissions, less the balance of your mortgage. This will help you develop a strategy for dealing with the lender.

Determine realistically whether your financial reversal is temporary or permanent. A temporary reversal is one where, if you are provided payment relief for up to 6 months, you will be able to resume regular payments at the end of the period, and repay all the payments you missed within the following 12 months. Set down the case for the reversal being temporary in writing.

If you can't meet these conditions, your financial reversal is considered permanent by the lender. If the change in your status is permanent, it means that you can resume regular payments only if the payment is permanently reduced. This requires modifying the loan contract: reducing the interest rate, extending the term or both.

You need to understand the position of the lender. While some actions you can take on your own, such as selling your house, other actions have to be negotiated with the lender. You do better in any negotiation if you know where the other party is coming from.

The lender's objective is to minimize loss. The action that minimizes loss to the lender depends on the equity in your house, on whether your financial reversal is temporary or permanent, and on whether or not you are dealing in good faith.

Substantial Equity. If you have substantial equity in your house, the least-costly action to the lender may be foreclosure. While foreclosure is costly, the lender is entitled to be reimbursed from the sales proceeds for all foreclosure costs plus all unpaid interest and principal.

While foreclosure makes the lender whole, it is a disaster for you. Your equity is depleted, you incur the costs of moving, and your credit is ruined. Hence, you must avoid foreclosure, if necessary by selling your house.

If your financial reversal is temporary, and you can persuade the lender of this, the lender may be willing to provide payment relief. The lender will probably prefer to keep your loan, rather than to foreclose on it, but only if it is a good loan. The burden of proof is on you in this situation to demonstrate that the relief will really work. It also helps if your state has an assistance program for borrowers experiencing mortgage hardship, which assumes some or all of the risk of providing payment relief.

If your financial reversal is permanent, sell the house before you begin accumulating delinquencies. In a high-equity situation, there is little hope that the lender will agree to modify the loan contract, so don't waste time trying. If you sell, at least you retain your equity and your credit rating.

Little or No Equity. *If your financial reversal is temporary* and you have little or no equity in your property, it will be easier to persuade the lender to offer payment relief. With no equity, the foreclosure alternative is more costly to the lender.

If your financial reversal is permanent, the lender probably will be willing to accept either a "short sale" or a "deed in lieu of foreclosure." In the first, you sell the house and pay the lender the sales proceeds while in the second the lender takes title to the house. In both cases your debt obligation usually is fully discharged. (They do appear on your credit report, but are not as bad a mark as a foreclosure.) The lender who can get all or most of his money back in these ways probably will not be willing to modify the loan contract.

The lender will turn a wary eye on borrowers who have the means to continue making payments but would like to rid themselves of their negative equity through short sale or deed-in-lieu. While these options are less costly to the lender than foreclosure, lenders view borrowers as responsible for their debt, regardless of the depletion of their equity. How they respond depends on how convinced they are that the borrower's problems are truly involuntary, and on the likelihood of success in collecting more if they elect to go after the borrower for the deficiency.

If your equity in the house is negative but you want to remain there, the lender may be favorably disposed to payment relief, or to contract modification if necessary to make the payment manageable. With negative equity, these may be the least-costly options for the lender.

59. How do I cancel private mortgage insurance?

Under one provision of federal legislation passed in 1999, lenders are required to cancel private mortgage insurance on most home mortgage loans made after July 29, 1999. Cancellation occurs automatically when amortization has reduced the loan balance to 78% of the value of the property at the time the loan was made.

But under another provision of this law, lenders must terminate insurance *at the borrower's request* when the loan balance hits 80% of the original value.

Borrowers who take the initiative can thus terminate earlier than those who wait.

Even under this provision, the wait can be a long one. With normal amortization, it takes 142 months for the loan balance on an 8% 30-year loan equal to 95% of the property value, to fall to 80%. A 15-year loan that is otherwise identical will get there in 47 months.

However, borrowers who add to their regular monthly payment will reach the 80% target more quickly. If they add 1/12 of the payment every month—for example, a $600 payment is raised to $650—the mortgages cited above will hit the 80% target in 91 months and 38 months, respectively.

Warning: The lender need not accept your request for cancellation if:

- You have a second mortgage.
- The property has declined in value.
- You had a payment late by 30 days or more within the year preceding the cancellation date, or late by 60 days or more in the year before that.

If your loan was made before July 29, 1999, you are not covered by this law. If it was sold to Fannie Mae or Freddie Mac, however, you are subject to the cancellation rules of the agencies regardless of when the loan was made. And these rules are more favorable to homeowners because they are based on the current appraised value of the property rather than the value at the time the loan was made. Under these rules:

- You can terminate after two years if the loan balance is no more than 75% of the current appraised value, and after 5 years if it is no more than 80%.
- You must request cancellation, and obtain an appraisal acceptable to the agencies and to the lender.
- The ratios required for termination are lower if

there is a second mortgage, if the property is held for investment rather than occupancy, or if the property is other than a single-family.

- The agencies will not accept termination if your payment has been 30-days late within the prior year, or 60-days late in the year before that.

Using current value rather than original value can substantially shorten the period to termination. For example, the 30-year 8% loan that takes 142 months to reach 80% of original value, will get there in 96 months with just 1% annual appreciation, and in 53 months with 3% appreciation.

If your loan was made before July 29, 1999, and if it is not held by Fannie or Freddie, the termination rules that apply are those of your lender. In some states (California, Connecticut, Maryland, Minnesota, Missouri, New York, North Carolina, Oregon, Texas, and Virginia), lenders' rules may be affected by state law.

The best strategy is to assume you are subject to the liberal Fannie/Freddie rules. After 2 years, begin periodically to estimate the current value of your house. Web sites offering tools that can help include Homegain.com, Dataquick.com, Propertyview.com, and Domania.com. Then you can use calculator 4a at www.mtgprofessor.com to see when you might be eligible. When it appears that you might meet the agencies' requirements, contact your lender and ask whether your mortgage is held by one of the agencies. If it is, confirm the ratio of balance to current value that permits termination in your case, and ask about acceptable appraisers.

If your loan isn't held by one of the agencies, ask the lender for a written statement of its own termination policy. If your loan was made after July 29, 1999, follow the more liberal of the lender's rules or the federal law. If your loan was made before July 29, 1999, you are stuck with the lender's rules.

But don't accept rules substantially less liberal than those of Fannie/Freddie without protest. Let the lender know that so long as you are forced to pay for insurance that Fannie Mae and Freddie Mac say isn't necessary, the lender need not try to cross-sell you anything else.

60. Is there recourse against bad servicing?

When a mortgage loan is closed, the origination file is closed and a servicing file is opened. It remains open for the life of the loan. Whether the process goes smoothly or badly depends on both the borrower and the servicing agent.

The servicing agent is the entity that receives the mortgage payment, keeps the payment records, provides borrowers with account statements, imposes late charges when the payment is late, and pursues delinquent borrowers. In many transactions, servicing agents also pay property taxes and insurance with money placed in escrow by the borrower.

Borrowers can choose from whom they borrow, but they can't choose the servicing agent. The agent may or may not be the lender who originated the loan. Servicing is frequently sold. Borrowers must be notified of transfers, but cannot prevent them.

My mail box is stuffed with letters from borrowers who complain about bad servicing. The following is a sample.

"My lender sold the loan and the new lender shortened the grace period and tripled the late fee...."

'My lender hit me with a late charge when my loan was paid on the 16th instead of the 15th, and for 7 months after that I have been hit with a late charge, even though all payments were made on time."

"My lender did not pay the taxes on time or for the correct amount...."

"My lender bought insurance on my house and added the premium to the loan balance, even though I already have insurance that I pay for...."

"My lender sends me statements that only show the payments, not the balance .... I have no idea how they are applying the payment."

Chuck Cross, a regulator for the state of Washington, has investigated numerous cases of this type. According to Cross, "about 50% of the time the consumer is wrong and has misread or misunderstood the process ... and in about 50% the lender has erred." In cases where the servicing agent is at fault, Cross does not know the extent to which the problems reflect deliberate attempts to generate more revenue, or innocent operating accidents. In either case, it is troubling that some of the names that pop up in my mail are among the largest and best known financial institutions in the country.

Since borrowers can't fire their servicing agents, what can they do to protect themselves? If you have been mistreated, you should file a written complaint with the lender addressed to customer service. Do not include it with your mortgage payment, which you should continue to make separately. State:

Your loan number

Names on loan documents

Property and/or mailing address

This is a "qualified written request" under Section 6 of the Real Estate Settlement Procedures Act (RESPA).

I am writing because:

[Describe the problem and the action you believe the lender should take.]

[Describe any previous attempts to resolve the issue, including conversations with customer service.]

[If it is relevant to the dispute, request a copy of your payment history.]

[List a day time telephone number.]

I understand that under Section 6 of RESPA you are required to acknowledge my request within 20 business days and must try to resolve the issue within 60 business days.

If this doesn't do the trick, you can file a complaint with HUD. You can also sue. According to HUD, "A borrower may bring a private law suit, or a group of borrowers may bring a class action suit, within three years, against a servicer who fails to comply with Section 6's provisions."

You can also file a complaint with the government agency that regulates the servicing agent. Here are Web sites you can use to contact these agencies:

- For national banks: **www.occ.treas.gov/customer.htm**
- For federally chartered savings and loan associations: **www.ots.treas.gov/contact.html**
- For state-chartered banks and savings and loans: **www.lendingprofessional.com/licensing.html**
- For mortgage banking firms: **www.aarmr.org/lists/members-IE.html**

If you don't know the proper agency, you can send the complaint to the consumer protection division of the state attorney general. It will be forwarded to the relevant state or federal agency.

Borrowers who are aware that they have a servicing problem might be the tip of the iceberg. All borrowers should periodically check their transaction history to make certain that a) payments are always applied to the balance at the end of the preceding month; b) tax and insurance payments from escrow are correct and there have been no double payments; c) rate adjustments on ARMs are in accordance with the method stipulated in the note; and d) there isn't anything in the history that looks "funny."

Any borrower who does not receive a complete transaction statement at least annually should periodically submit a "qualified written request" for one using the form described above.

Appendix A

Monthly Payment Tables

What is the monthly payment?

All mortgages in the United States have a monthly mortgage payment of principal and interest. In most cases, this is the payment the borrower is obliged to make every month. In a few cases, the monthly payment is divided in half, and the borrower pays half every two weeks (a "biweekly"), or twice a month (a "bimonthly"). But even in these cases, a monthly payment is calculated as the first step.

The monthly payment has two components: interest and principal. In each month, the interest is calculated by dividing the rate by 12, and multiplying it times the loan balance in the preceding month. For example, if the rate is 6% and the loan balance is $100,000, the interest payment for that month is .06/12 times $100,000, or $500. The principal is the payment less the interest. If the payment is $600 in the example, the principal is $100.

Since each payment of principal reduces the loan balance by the same amount, interest payments decline over time, and principal payments rise. The pace of repayment quickens as the mortgage ages.

The monthly payments shown here are "fully amortizing." This means that if they are continued through the life of the loan, the balance will be extinguished with the final payment.

Not all payments are fully amortizing, especially on

adjustable rate mortgages (ARMs). Some payments are interest only for a period. The principal payment is zero, so the loan balance does not change. In other ARMs, the payment is actually less than the interest for a period, so the principal payment is negative. It adds to the loan balance, rather than reducing it, referred to as "negative amortization." The tables do not cover these exotic cases.

Finding the Monthly Payment: Example 1

The Goldblatts are borrowing $180,000 for 15 years at 5.5%. To find their monthly payment, go to the page that covers a 5.5% interest rate, run down the left-hand column to $180,000, then on the same line go to the second column headed 15 years. The payment is $1470.76.

Adding and Subtracting Payments: Example 2

The Ferguson's are also borrowing for 15 years at 5.5%, but their loan is $182,000, which is not shown on the table. In this case, add the $1470.76 payment on $180,000 to the $16.35 payment on $2,000, resulting in a payment of $1487.11 on $182,000.

You will get the same result if you subtract the payment of $65.37 on $8,000 from the payment of $1552.46 on $190,000. Don't worry about a difference of a penny or two, it arises because of rounding.

Multiplying Payments: Example 3

The Smiths are borrowing for 15 years at 5.5%, but their $600,000 loan goes beyond the limits of the table. In this case, multiply the $2451.26 payment on $300,000 by 2, which results in a payment of $4902.52. You will also get this result if you multiply the $1634.17 payment on $200,000 by 3.

Rate Interpolation: The Johnsons are borrowing $100,000 for 15 years at 5.125%, a rate that is not shown in the tables. In this situation, the payment will be approximately equal to the average of the payment of $790.80 at 5%, and the payment of $803.88 at 5.25%. Adding them and dividing by 2 you get $797.34. Any error will be no more than a few pennies.

Total Interest: The monthly payment tables can be used to calculate the total amount of interest you will pay over the life of the loan, assuming the loan has a fixed interest rate and you hold it to term. Since the total of all principal payments equals the loan amount, deducting the loan amount from the total payments will leave the total interest payments.

For example, the Goldblatts will pay $ 1470.76 for 15 years. Multiplying $1470.76 times 180 gives total payments of $264,736.80. Subtracting the loan amount of $180,000 results in interest payments of $84,736.80.

With an interest rate of 4.00%, your monthly payment will be:

Loan Amount	Number of Years in Term				
	10	15	20	25	30
$1,000	$10.13	$7.40	$6.06	$5.28	$4.78
$2,000	$20.25	$14.80	$12.12	$10.56	$9.55
$3,000	$30.38	$22.20	$18.18	$15.84	$14.33
$4,000	$40.50	$29.59	$24.24	$21.12	$19.10
$5,000	$50.63	$36.99	$30.30	$26.40	$23.88
$6,000	$60.75	$44.39	$36.36	$31.68	$28.65
$7,000	$70.88	$51.78	$42.42	$36.95	$33.42
$8,000	$81.00	$59.18	$48.48	$42.23	$38.20
$9,000	$91.13	$66.58	$54.54	$47.51	$42.97
$10,000	$101.25	$73.97	$60.60	$52.79	$47.75
$15,000	$151.87	$110.96	$90.90	$79.18	$71.62
$20,000	$202.50	$147.94	$121.20	$105.57	$95.49
$25,000	$253.12	$184.93	$151.50	$131.96	$119.36
$30,000	$303.74	$221.91	$181.80	$158.36	$143.23
$35,000	$354.36	$258.90	$212.10	$184.75	$167.10
$40,000	$404.99	$295.88	$242.40	$211.14	$190.97
$45,000	$455.61	$332.86	$272.70	$237.53	$214.84
$50,000	$506.23	$369.85	$303.00	$263.92	$238.71
$55,000	$556.85	$406.83	$333.29	$290.32	$262.58
$60,000	$607.48	$443.82	$363.59	$316.71	$286.45
$65,000	$658.10	$480.80	$393.89	$343.10	$310.32
$70,000	$708.72	$517.79	$424.19	$369.49	$334.20
$75,000	$759.34	$554.77	$454.49	$395.88	$358.07
$80,000	$809.97	$591.76	$484.79	$422.27	$381.94
$85,000	$860.59	$628.74	$515.09	$448.67	$405.81
$90,000	$911.21	$665.72	$545.39	$475.06	$429.68
$95,000	$961.83	$702.71	$575.69	$501.45	$453.55
$100,000	$1,012.46	$739.69	$605.99	$527.84	$477.42
$110,000	$1,113.70	$813.66	$666.58	$580.63	$525.16
$120,000	$1,214.95	$887.63	$727.18	$633.41	$572.90
$125,000	$1,265.57	$924.61	$757.48	$659.80	$596.77
$130,000	$1,316.19	$961.60	$787.78	$686.19	$620.64
$140,000	$1,417.44	$1,035.57	$848.38	$738.98	$668.39
$150,000	$1,518.68	$1,109.54	$908.98	$791.76	$716.13
$160,000	$1,619.93	$1,183.51	$969.57	$844.54	$763.87
$170,000	$1,721.17	$1,257.47	$1,030.17	$897.33	$811.61
$175,000	$1,771.79	$1,294.46	$1,060.47	$923.72	$835.48
$180,000	$1,822.42	$1,331.44	$1,090.77	$950.11	$859.35
$190,000	$1,923.66	$1,405.41	$1,151.37	$1,002.89	$907.09
$200,000	$2,024.91	$1,479.38	$1,211.97	$1,055.68	$954.84
$210,000	$2,126.15	$1,553.35	$1,272.56	$1,108.46	$1,002.58
$220,000	$2,227.40	$1,627.32	$1,333.16	$1,161.25	$1,050.32
$225,000	$2,278.02	$1,664.30	$1,363.46	$1,187.64	$1,074.19
$230,000	$2,328.64	$1,701.29	$1,393.76	$1,214.03	$1,098.06
$240,000	$2,429.89	$1,775.26	$1,454.36	$1,266.81	$1,145.80
$250,000	$2,531.13	$1,849.22	$1,514.96	$1,319.60	$1,193.54
$260,000	$2,632.38	$1,923.19	$1,575.55	$1,372.38	$1,241.28
$270,000	$2,733.62	$1,997.16	$1,636.15	$1,425.16	$1,289.03
$275,000	$2,784.25	$2,034.15	$1,666.45	$1,451.56	$1,312.90
$280,000	$2,834.87	$2,071.13	$1,696.75	$1,477.95	$1,336.77
$290,000	$2,936.11	$2,145.10	$1,757.35	$1,530.73	$1,384.51
$300,000	$3,037.36	$2,219.07	$1,817.95	$1,583.52	$1,432.25

With an interest rate of 4.00%, your monthly payment will be:

Loan Amount	Number of Years in Term				
	10	15	20	25	30
$310,000	$3,138.60	$2,293.04	$1,878.54	$1,636.30	$1,479.99
$320,000	$3,239.85	$2,367.01	$1,939.14	$1,689.08	$1,527.73
$325,000	$3,290.47	$2,403.99	$1,969.44	$1,715.47	$1,551.60
$330,000	$3,341.09	$2,440.98	$1,999.74	$1,741.87	$1,575.48
$340,000	$3,442.34	$2,514.94	$2,060.34	$1,794.65	$1,623.22
$350,000	$3,543.58	$2,588.91	$2,120.94	$1,847.43	$1,670.96
$360,000	$3,644.83	$2,662.88	$2,181.53	$1,900.22	$1,718.70
$370,000	$3,746.08	$2,736.85	$2,242.13	$1,953.00	$1,766.44
$375,000	$3,796.70	$2,773.83	$2,272.43	$1,979.39	$1,790.31
$380,000	$3,847.32	$2,810.82	$2,302.73	$2,005.78	$1,814.18
$390,000	$3,948.57	$2,884.79	$2,363.33	$2,058.57	$1,861.92
$400,000	$4,049.81	$2,958.76	$2,423.93	$2,111.35	$1,909.67

With an interest rate of 4.25%, your monthly payment will be:

Loan Amount	Number of Years in Term				
	10	15	20	25	30
$1,000	$10.25	$7.53	$6.20	$5.42	$4.92
$2,000	$20.49	$15.05	$12.39	$10.84	$9.84
$3,000	$30.74	$22.57	$18.58	$16.26	$14.76
$4,000	$40.98	$30.10	$24.77	$21.67	$19.68
$5,000	$51.22	$37.62	$30.97	$27.09	$24.60
$6,000	$61.47	$45.14	$37.16	$32.51	$29.52
$7,000	$71.71	$52.66	$43.35	$37.93	$34.44
$8,000	$81.96	$60.19	$49.54	$43.34	$39.36
$9,000	$92.20	$67.71	$55.74	$48.76	$44.28
$10,000	$102.44	$75.23	$61.93	$54.18	$49.20
$15,000	$153.66	$112.85	$92.89	$81.27	$73.80
$20,000	$204.88	$150.46	$123.85	$108.35	$98.39
$25,000	$256.10	$188.07	$154.81	$135.44	$122.99
$30,000	$307.32	$225.69	$185.78	$162.53	$147.59
$35,000	$358.54	$263.30	$216.74	$189.61	$172.18
$40,000	$409.76	$300.92	$247.70	$216.70	$196.78
$45,000	$460.97	$338.53	$278.66	$243.79	$221.38
$50,000	$512.19	$376.14	$309.62	$270.87	$245.97
$55,000	$563.41	$413.76	$340.58	$297.96	$270.57
$60,000	$614.63	$451.37	$371.55	$325.05	$295.17
$65,000	$665.85	$488.99	$402.51	$352.13	$319.77
$70,000	$717.07	$526.60	$433.47	$379.22	$344.36
$75,000	$768.29	$564.21	$464.43	$406.31	$368.96
$80,000	$819.51	$601.83	$495.39	$433.40	$393.56
$85,000	$870.72	$639.44	$526.35	$460.48	$418.15
$90,000	$921.94	$677.06	$557.32	$487.57	$442.75
$95,000	$973.16	$714.67	$588.28	$514.66	$467.35
$100,000	$1,024.38	$752.28	$619.24	$541.74	$491.94
$110,000	$1,126.82	$827.51	$681.16	$595.92	$541.14
$120,000	$1,229.26	$902.74	$743.09	$650.09	$590.33
$125,000	$1,280.47	$940.35	$774.05	$677.18	$614.93
$130,000	$1,331.69	$977.97	$805.01	$704.26	$639.53
$140,000	$1,434.13	$1,053.19	$866.93	$758.44	$688.72
$150,000	$1,536.57	$1,128.42	$928.86	$812.61	$737.91

With an interest rate of 4.25%, your monthly payment will be:

Loan Amount	Number of Years in Term				
	10	15	20	25	30
$160,000	$1,639.01	$1,203.65	$990.78	$866.79	$787.11
$170,000	$1,741.44	$1,278.88	$1,052.70	$920.96	$836.30
$175,000	$1,792.66	$1,316.49	$1,083.67	$948.05	$860.90
$180,000	$1,843.88	$1,354.11	$1,114.63	$975.13	$885.50
$190,000	$1,946.32	$1,429.33	$1,176.55	$1,029.31	$934.69
$200,000	$2,048.76	$1,504.56	$1,238.47	$1,083.48	$983.88
$210,000	$2,151.19	$1,579.79	$1,300.40	$1,137.66	$1,033.08
$220,000	$2,253.63	$1,655.02	$1,362.32	$1,191.83	$1,082.27
$225,000	$2,304.85	$1,692.63	$1,393.28	$1,218.92	$1,106.87
$230,000	$2,356.07	$1,730.25	$1,424.24	$1,246.00	$1,131.47
$240,000	$2,458.51	$1,805.47	$1,486.17	$1,300.18	$1,180.66
$250,000	$2,560.94	$1,880.70	$1,548.09	$1,354.35	$1,229.85
$260,000	$2,663.38	$1,955.93	$1,610.01	$1,408.52	$1,279.05
$270,000	$2,765.82	$2,031.16	$1,671.94	$1,462.70	$1,328.24
$275,000	$2,817.04	$2,068.77	$1,702.90	$1,489.78	$1,352.84
$280,000	$2,868.26	$2,106.38	$1,733.86	$1,516.87	$1,377.44
$290,000	$2,970.69	$2,181.61	$1,795.78	$1,571.05	$1,426.63
$300,000	$3,073.13	$2,256.84	$1,857.71	$1,625.22	$1,475.82
$310,000	$3,175.57	$2,332.07	$1,919.63	$1,679.39	$1,525.02
$320,000	$3,278.01	$2,407.30	$1,981.56	$1,733.57	$1,574.21
$325,000	$3,329.22	$2,444.91	$2,012.52	$1,760.65	$1,598.81
$330,000	$3,380.44	$2,482.52	$2,043.48	$1,787.74	$1,623.41
$340,000	$3,482.88	$2,557.75	$2,105.40	$1,841.91	$1,672.60
$350,000	$3,585.32	$2,632.98	$2,167.33	$1,896.09	$1,721.79
$360,000	$3,687.76	$2,708.21	$2,229.25	$1,950.26	$1,770.99
$370,000	$3,790.19	$2,783.44	$2,291.17	$2,004.44	$1,820.18
$375,000	$3,841.41	$2,821.05	$2,322.13	$2,031.52	$1,844.78
$380,000	$3,892.63	$2,858.66	$2,353.10	$2,058.61	$1,869.38
$390,000	$3,995.07	$2,933.89	$2,415.02	$2,112.78	$1,918.57
$400,000	$4,097.51	$3,009.12	$2,476.94	$2,166.96	$1,967.76

With an interest rate of 4.5%, your monthly payment will be:

Loan Amount	Number of Years in Term				
	10	15	20	25	30
$1,000	$10.37	$7.65	$6.33	$5.56	$5.07
$2,000	$20.73	$15.30	$12.66	$11.12	$10.14
$3,000	$31.10	$22.95	$18.98	$16.68	$15.21
$4,000	$41.46	$30.60	$25.31	$22.24	$20.27
$5,000	$51.82	$38.25	$31.64	$27.80	$25.34
$6,000	$62.19	$45.90	$37.96	$33.35	$30.41
$7,000	$72.55	$53.55	$44.29	$38.91	$35.47
$8,000	$82.92	$61.20	$50.62	$44.47	$40.54
$9,000	$93.28	$68.85	$56.94	$50.03	$45.61
$10,000	$103.64	$76.50	$63.27	$55.59	$50.67
$15,000	$155.46	$114.75	$94.90	$83.38	$76.01
$20,000	$207.28	$153.00	$126.53	$111.17	$101.34
$25,000	$259.10	$191.25	$158.17	$138.96	$126.68
$30,000	$310.92	$229.50	$189.80	$166.75	$152.01

With an interest rate of 4.5%, your monthly payment will be:

Loan Amount	Number of Years in Term				
	10	15	20	25	30
$35,000	$362.74	$267.75	$221.43	$194.55	$177.34
$40,000	$414.56	$306.00	$253.06	$222.34	$202.68
$45,000	$466.38	$344.25	$284.70	$250.13	$228.01
$50,000	$518.20	$382.50	$316.33	$277.92	$253.35
$55,000	$570.02	$420.75	$347.96	$305.71	$278.68
$60,000	$621.84	$459.00	$379.59	$333.50	$304.02
$65,000	$673.65	$497.25	$411.23	$361.30	$329.35
$70,000	$725.47	$535.50	$442.86	$389.09	$354.68
$75,000	$777.29	$573.75	$474.49	$416.88	$380.02
$80,000	$829.11	$612.00	$506.12	$444.67	$405.35
$85,000	$880.93	$650.25	$537.76	$472.46	$430.69
$90,000	$932.75	$688.50	$569.39	$500.25	$456.02
$95,000	$984.57	$726.75	$601.02	$528.05	$481.36
$100,000	$1,036.39	$765.00	$632.65	$555.84	$506.69
$110,000	$1,140.03	$841.50	$695.92	$611.42	$557.36
$120,000	$1,243.67	$918.00	$759.18	$667.00	$608.03
$125,000	$1,295.49	$956.25	$790.82	$694.80	$633.36
$130,000	$1,347.30	$994.50	$822.45	$722.59	$658.70
$140,000	$1,450.94	$1,071.00	$885.71	$778.17	$709.36
$150,000	$1,554.58	$1,147.49	$948.98	$833.75	$760.03
$160,000	$1,658.22	$1,223.99	$1,012.24	$889.34	$810.70
$170,000	$1,761.86	$1,300.49	$1,075.51	$944.92	$861.37
$175,000	$1,813.68	$1,338.74	$1,107.14	$972.71	$886.70
$180,000	$1,865.50	$1,376.99	$1,138.77	$1,000.50	$912.04
$190,000	$1,969.13	$1,453.49	$1,202.04	$1,056.09	$962.71
$200,000	$2,072.77	$1,529.99	$1,265.30	$1,111.67	$1,013.38
$210,000	$2,176.41	$1,606.49	$1,328.57	$1,167.25	$1,064.04
$220,000	$2,280.05	$1,682.99	$1,391.83	$1,222.84	$1,114.71
$225,000	$2,331.87	$1,721.24	$1,423.47	$1,250.63	$1,140.05
$230,000	$2,383.69	$1,759.49	$1,455.10	$1,278.42	$1,165.38
$240,000	$2,487.33	$1,835.99	$1,518.36	$1,334.00	$1,216.05
$250,000	$2,590.97	$1,912.49	$1,581.63	$1,389.59	$1,266.72
$260,000	$2,694.60	$1,988.99	$1,644.89	$1,445.17	$1,317.39
$270,000	$2,798.24	$2,065.49	$1,708.16	$1,500.75	$1,368.06
$275,000	$2,850.06	$2,103.74	$1,739.79	$1,528.54	$1,393.39
$280,000	$2,901.88	$2,141.99	$1,771.42	$1,556.34	$1,418.72
$290,000	$3,005.52	$2,218.49	$1,834.69	$1,611.92	$1,469.39
$300,000	$3,109.16	$2,294.98	$1,897.95	$1,667.50	$1,520.06
$310,000	$3,212.80	$2,371.48	$1,961.22	$1,723.09	$1,570.73
$320,000	$3,316.43	$2,447.98	$2,024.48	$1,778.67	$1,621.40
$325,000	$3,368.25	$2,486.23	$2,056.12	$1,806.46	$1,646.73
$330,000	$3,420.07	$2,524.48	$2,087.75	$1,834.25	$1,672.07
$340,000	$3,523.71	$2,600.98	$2,151.01	$1,889.84	$1,722.74
$350,000	$3,627.35	$2,677.48	$2,214.28	$1,945.42	$1,773.40
$360,000	$3,730.99	$2,753.98	$2,277.54	$2,001.00	$1,824.07
$370,000	$3,834.63	$2,830.48	$2,340.81	$2,056.59	$1,874.74
$375,000	$3,886.45	$2,868.73	$2,372.44	$2,084.38	$1,900.07
$380,000	$3,938.26	$2,906.98	$2,404.07	$2,112.17	$1,925.41
$390,000	$4,041.90	$2,983.48	$2,467.34	$2,167.75	$1,976.08
$400,000	$4,145.54	$3,059.98	$2,530.60	$2,223.33	$2,026.75

With an interest rate of 4.75%, your monthly payment will be:

Loan Amount	Number of Years in Term				
	10	***15***	***20***	***25***	***30***
$1,000	$10.49	$7.78	$6.47	$5.71	$5.22
$2,000	$20.97	$15.56	$12.93	$11.41	$10.44
$3,000	$31.46	$23.34	$19.39	$17.11	$15.65
$4,000	$41.94	$31.12	$25.85	$22.81	$20.87
$5,000	$52.43	$38.90	$32.32	$28.51	$26.09
$6,000	$62.91	$46.67	$38.78	$34.21	$31.30
$7,000	$73.40	$54.45	$45.24	$39.91	$36.52
$8,000	$83.88	$62.23	$51.70	$45.61	$41.74
$9,000	$94.37	$70.01	$58.17	$51.32	$46.95
$10,000	$104.85	$77.79	$64.63	$57.02	$52.17
$15,000	$157.28	$116.68	$96.94	$85.52	$78.25
$20,000	$209.70	$155.57	$129.25	$114.03	$104.33
$25,000	$262.12	$194.46	$161.56	$142.53	$130.42
$30,000	$314.55	$233.35	$193.87	$171.04	$156.50
$35,000	$366.97	$272.25	$226.18	$199.55	$182.58
$40,000	$419.40	$311.14	$258.49	$228.05	$208.66
$45,000	$471.82	$350.03	$290.81	$256.56	$234.75
$50,000	$524.24	$388.92	$323.12	$285.06	$260.83
$55,000	$576.67	$427.81	$355.43	$313.57	$286.91
$60,000	$629.09	$466.70	$387.74	$342.08	$312.99
$65,000	$681.52	$505.60	$420.05	$370.58	$339.08
$70,000	$733.94	$544.49	$452.36	$399.09	$365.16
$75,000	$786.36	$583.38	$484.67	$427.59	$391.24
$80,000	$838.79	$622.27	$516.98	$456.10	$417.32
$85,000	$891.21	$661.16	$549.30	$484.60	$443.41
$90,000	$943.63	$700.05	$581.61	$513.11	$469.49
$95,000	$996.06	$738.95	$613.92	$541.62	$495.57
$100,000	$1,048.48	$777.84	$646.23	$570.12	$521.65
$110,000	$1,153.33	$855.62	$710.85	$627.13	$573.82
$120,000	$1,258.18	$933.40	$775.47	$684.15	$625.98
$125,000	$1,310.60	$972.29	$807.78	$712.65	$652.06
$130,000	$1,363.03	$1,011.19	$840.10	$741.16	$678.15
$140,000	$1,467.87	$1,088.97	$904.72	$798.17	$730.31
$150,000	$1,572.72	$1,166.75	$969.34	$855.18	$782.48
$160,000	$1,677.57	$1,244.54	$1,033.96	$912.19	$834.64
$170,000	$1,782.42	$1,322.32	$1,098.59	$969.20	$886.81
$175,000	$1,834.84	$1,361.21	$1,130.90	$997.71	$912.89
$180,000	$1,887.26	$1,400.10	$1,163.21	$1,026.22	$938.97
$190,000	$1,992.11	$1,477.89	$1,227.83	$1,083.23	$991.13
$200,000	$2,096.96	$1,555.67	$1,292.45	$1,140.24	$1,043.30
$210,000	$2,201.81	$1,633.45	$1,357.07	$1,197.25	$1,095.46
$220,000	$2,306.66	$1,711.24	$1,421.70	$1,254.26	$1,147.63
$225,000	$2,359.08	$1,750.13	$1,454.01	$1,282.77	$1,173.71
$230,000	$2,411.50	$1,789.02	$1,486.32	$1,311.27	$1,199.79
$240,000	$2,516.35	$1,866.80	$1,550.94	$1,368.29	$1,251.96
$250,000	$2,621.20	$1,944.58	$1,615.56	$1,425.30	$1,304.12
$260,000	$2,726.05	$2,022.37	$1,680.19	$1,482.31	$1,356.29
$270,000	$2,830.89	$2,100.15	$1,744.81	$1,539.32	$1,408.45
$275,000	$2,883.32	$2,139.04	$1,777.12	$1,567.83	$1,434.54
$280,000	$2,935.74	$2,177.93	$1,809.43	$1,596.33	$1,460.62
$290,000	$3,040.59	$2,255.72	$1,874.05	$1,653.35	$1,512.78
$300,000	$3,145.44	$2,333.50	$1,938.68	$1,710.36	$1,564.95

With an interest rate of 4.75%, your monthly payment will be:

Loan Amount	Number of Years in Term				
	10	15	20	25	30
$310,000	$3,250.29	$2,411.28	$2,003.30	$1,767.37	$1,617.11
$320,000	$3,355.13	$2,489.07	$2,067.92	$1,824.38	$1,669.28
$325,000	$3,407.56	$2,527.96	$2,100.23	$1,852.89	$1,695.36
$330,000	$3,459.98	$2,566.85	$2,132.54	$1,881.39	$1,721.44
$340,000	$3,564.83	$2,644.63	$2,197.17	$1,938.40	$1,773.61
$350,000	$3,669.68	$2,722.42	$2,261.79	$1,995.42	$1,825.77
$360,000	$3,774.52	$2,800.20	$2,326.41	$2,052.43	$1,877.94
$370,000	$3,879.37	$2,877.98	$2,391.03	$2,109.44	$1,930.10
$375,000	$3,931.80	$2,916.87	$2,423.34	$2,137.95	$1,956.18
$380,000	$3,984.22	$2,955.77	$2,455.65	$2,166.45	$1,982.26
$390,000	$4,089.07	$3,033.55	$2,520.28	$2,223.46	$2,034.43
$400,000	$4,193.91	$3,111.33	$2,584.90	$2,280.47	$2,086.59

With an interest rate of 5.00%, your monthly payment will be:

Loan Amount	Number of Years in Term				
	10	15	20	25	30
$1,000	$10.61	$7.91	$6.60	$5.85	$5.37
$2,000	$21.22	$15.82	$13.20	$11.70	$10.74
$3,000	$31.82	$23.73	$19.80	$17.54	$16.11
$4,000	$42.43	$31.64	$26.40	$23.39	$21.48
$5,000	$53.04	$39.54	$33.00	$29.23	$26.85
$6,000	$63.64	$47.45	$39.60	$35.08	$32.21
$7,000	$74.25	$55.36	$46.20	$40.93	$37.58
$8,000	$84.86	$63.27	$52.80	$46.77	$42.95
$9,000	$95.46	$71.18	$59.40	$52.62	$48.32
$10,000	$106.07	$79.08	$66.00	$58.46	$53.69
$15,000	$159.10	$118.62	$99.00	$87.69	$80.53
$20,000	$212.14	$158.16	$132.00	$116.92	$107.37
$25,000	$265.17	$197.70	$164.99	$146.15	$134.21
$30,000	$318.20	$237.24	$197.99	$175.38	$161.05
$35,000	$371.23	$276.78	$230.99	$204.61	$187.89
$40,000	$424.27	$316.32	$263.99	$233.84	$214.73
$45,000	$477.30	$355.86	$296.99	$263.07	$241.57
$50,000	$530.33	$395.40	$329.98	$292.30	$268.42
$55,000	$583.37	$434.94	$362.98	$321.53	$295.26
$60,000	$636.40	$474.48	$395.98	$350.76	$322.10
$65,000	$689.43	$514.02	$428.98	$379.99	$348.94
$70,000	$742.46	$553.56	$461.97	$409.22	$375.78
$75,000	$795.50	$593.10	$494.97	$438.45	$402.62
$80,000	$848.53	$632.64	$527.97	$467.68	$429.46
$85,000	$901.56	$672.18	$560.97	$496.91	$456.30
$90,000	$954.59	$711.72	$593.97	$526.14	$483.14
$95,000	$1,007.63	$751.26	$626.96	$555.37	$509.99
$100,000	$1,060.66	$790.80	$659.96	$584.60	$536.83
$110,000	$1,166.73	$869.88	$725.96	$643.05	$590.51
$120,000	$1,272.79	$948.96	$791.95	$701.51	$644.19
$125,000	$1,325.82	$988.50	$824.95	$730.74	$671.03
$130,000	$1,378.86	$1,028.04	$857.95	$759.97	$697.87
$140,000	$1,484.92	$1,107.12	$923.94	$818.43	$751.56
$150,000	$1,590.99	$1,186.20	$989.94	$876.89	$805.24

With an interest rate of 5.00%, your monthly payment will be:

Loan Amount	Number of Years in Term				
	10	15	20	25	30
$160,000	$1,697.05	$1,265.27	$1,055.93	$935.35	$858.92
$170,000	$1,803.12	$1,344.35	$1,121.93	$993.81	$912.60
$175,000	$1,856.15	$1,383.89	$1,154.93	$1,023.04	$939.44
$180,000	$1,909.18	$1,423.43	$1,187.93	$1,052.27	$966.28
$190,000	$2,015.25	$1,502.51	$1,253.92	$1,110.73	$1,019.97
$200,000	$2,121.32	$1,581.59	$1,319.92	$1,169.19	$1,073.65
$210,000	$2,227.38	$1,660.67	$1,385.91	$1,227.64	$1,127.33
$220,000	$2,333.45	$1,739.75	$1,451.91	$1,286.10	$1,181.01
$225,000	$2,386.48	$1,779.29	$1,484.91	$1,315.33	$1,207.85
$230,000	$2,439.51	$1,818.83	$1,517.90	$1,344.56	$1,234.69
$240,000	$2,545.58	$1,897.91	$1,583.90	$1,403.02	$1,288.38
$250,000	$2,651.64	$1,976.99	$1,649.89	$1,461.48	$1,342.06
$260,000	$2,757.71	$2,056.07	$1,715.89	$1,519.94	$1,395.74
$270,000	$2,863.77	$2,135.15	$1,781.89	$1,578.40	$1,449.42
$275,000	$2,916.81	$2,174.69	$1,814.88	$1,607.63	$1,476.26
$280,000	$2,969.84	$2,214.23	$1,847.88	$1,636.86	$1,503.11
$290,000	$3,075.90	$2,293.31	$1,913.88	$1,695.32	$1,556.79
$300,000	$3,181.97	$2,372.39	$1,979.87	$1,753.78	$1,610.47
$310,000	$3,288.04	$2,451.47	$2,045.87	$1,812.23	$1,664.15
$320,000	$3,394.10	$2,530.54	$2,111.86	$1,870.69	$1,717.83
$325,000	$3,447.13	$2,570.08	$2,144.86	$1,899.92	$1,744.68
$330,000	$3,500.17	$2,609.62	$2,177.86	$1,929.15	$1,771.52
$340,000	$3,606.23	$2,688.70	$2,243.85	$1,987.61	$1,825.20
$350,000	$3,712.30	$2,767.78	$2,309.85	$2,046.07	$1,878.88
$360,000	$3,818.36	$2,846.86	$2,375.85	$2,104.53	$1,932.56
$370,000	$3,924.43	$2,925.94	$2,441.84	$2,162.99	$1,986.25
$375,000	$3,977.46	$2,965.48	$2,474.84	$2,192.22	$2,013.09
$380,000	$4,030.49	$3,005.02	$2,507.84	$2,221.45	$2,039.93
$390,000	$4,136.56	$3,084.10	$2,573.83	$2,279.91	$2,093.61
$400,000	$4,242.63	$3,163.18	$2,639.83	$2,338.37	$2,147.29

With an interest rate of 5.25%, your monthly payment will be:

Loan Amount	Number of Years in Term				
	10	15	20	25	30
$1,000	$10.73	$8.04	$6.74	$6.00	$5.53
$2,000	$21.46	$16.08	$13.48	$11.99	$11.05
$3,000	$32.19	$24.12	$20.22	$17.98	$16.57
$4,000	$42.92	$32.16	$26.96	$23.97	$22.09
$5,000	$53.65	$40.20	$33.70	$29.97	$27.62
$6,000	$64.38	$48.24	$40.44	$35.96	$33.14
$7,000	$75.11	$56.28	$47.17	$41.95	$38.66
$8,000	$85.84	$64.32	$53.91	$47.94	$44.18
$9,000	$96.57	$72.35	$60.65	$53.94	$49.70
$10,000	$107.30	$80.39	$67.39	$59.93	$55.23
$15,000	$160.94	$120.59	$101.08	$89.89	$82.84
$20,000	$214.59	$160.78	$134.77	$119.85	$110.45
$25,000	$268.23	$200.97	$168.47	$149.82	$138.06
$30,000	$321.88	$241.17	$202.16	$179.78	$165.67

With an interest rate of 5.25%, your monthly payment will be:

Loan Amount	Number of Years in Term				
	10	15	20	25	30
$35,000	$375.53	$281.36	$235.85	$209.74	$193.28
$40,000	$429.17	$321.56	$269.54	$239.70	$220.89
$45,000	$482.82	$361.75	$303.23	$269.67	$248.50
$50,000	$536.46	$401.94	$336.93	$299.63	$276.11
$55,000	$590.11	$442.14	$370.62	$329.59	$303.72
$60,000	$643.76	$482.33	$404.31	$359.55	$331.33
$65,000	$697.40	$522.53	$438.00	$389.52	$358.94
$70,000	$751.05	$562.72	$471.70	$419.48	$386.55
$75,000	$804.69	$602.91	$505.39	$449.44	$414.16
$80,000	$858.34	$643.11	$539.08	$479.40	$441.77
$85,000	$911.98	$683.30	$572.77	$509.37	$469.38
$90,000	$965.63	$723.49	$606.46	$539.33	$496.99
$95,000	$1,019.28	$763.69	$640.16	$569.29	$524.60
$100,000	$1,072.92	$803.88	$673.85	$599.25	$552.21
$110,000	$1,180.21	$884.27	$741.23	$659.18	$607.43
$120,000	$1,287.51	$964.66	$808.62	$719.10	$662.65
$125,000	$1,341.15	$1,004.85	$842.31	$749.06	$690.26
$130,000	$1,394.80	$1,045.05	$876.00	$779.03	$717.87
$140,000	$1,502.09	$1,125.43	$943.39	$838.95	$773.09
$150,000	$1,609.38	$1,205.82	$1,010.77	$898.88	$828.31
$160,000	$1,716.67	$1,286.21	$1,078.16	$958.80	$883.53
$170,000	$1,823.96	$1,366.60	$1,145.54	$1,018.73	$938.75
$175,000	$1,877.61	$1,406.79	$1,179.23	$1,048.69	$966.36
$180,000	$1,931.26	$1,446.98	$1,212.92	$1,078.65	$993.97
$190,000	$2,038.55	$1,527.37	$1,280.31	$1,138.58	$1,049.19
$200,000	$2,145.84	$1,607.76	$1,347.69	$1,198.50	$1,104.41
$210,000	$2,253.13	$1,688.15	$1,415.08	$1,258.43	$1,159.63
$220,000	$2,360.42	$1,768.54	$1,482.46	$1,318.35	$1,214.85
$225,000	$2,414.07	$1,808.73	$1,516.15	$1,348.31	$1,242.46
$230,000	$2,467.71	$1,848.92	$1,549.85	$1,378.27	$1,270.07
$240,000	$2,575.01	$1,929.31	$1,617.23	$1,438.20	$1,325.29
$250,000	$2,682.30	$2,009.70	$1,684.62	$1,498.12	$1,380.51
$260,000	$2,789.59	$2,090.09	$1,752.00	$1,558.05	$1,435.73
$270,000	$2,896.88	$2,170.47	$1,819.38	$1,617.97	$1,490.95
$275,000	$2,950.53	$2,210.67	$1,853.08	$1,647.94	$1,518.57
$280,000	$3,004.17	$2,250.86	$1,886.77	$1,677.90	$1,546.18
$290,000	$3,111.46	$2,331.25	$1,954.15	$1,737.82	$1,601.40
$300,000	$3,218.76	$2,411.64	$2,021.54	$1,797.75	$1,656.62
$310,000	$3,326.05	$2,492.03	$2,088.92	$1,857.67	$1,711.84
$320,000	$3,433.34	$2,572.41	$2,156.31	$1,917.60	$1,767.06
$325,000	$3,486.99	$2,612.61	$2,190.00	$1,947.56	$1,794.67
$330,000	$3,540.63	$2,652.80	$2,223.69	$1,977.52	$1,822.28
$340,000	$3,647.92	$2,733.19	$2,291.08	$2,037.45	$1,877.50
$350,000	$3,755.21	$2,813.58	$2,358.46	$2,097.37	$1,932.72
$360,000	$3,862.51	$2,893.96	$2,425.84	$2,157.30	$1,987.94
$370,000	$3,969.80	$2,974.35	$2,493.23	$2,217.22	$2,043.16
$375,000	$4,023.44	$3,014.55	$2,526.92	$2,247.18	$2,070.77
$380,000	$4,077.09	$3,054.74	$2,560.61	$2,277.15	$2,098.38
$390,000	$4,184.38	$3,135.13	$2,628.00	$2,337.07	$2,153.60
$400,000	$4,291.67	$3,215.52	$2,695.38	$2,397.00	$2,208.82

With an interest rate of 5.5%, your monthly payment will be:

Loan Amount	Number of Years in Term				
	10	15	20	25	30
$1,000	$10.86	$8.18	$6.88	$6.15	$5.68
$2,000	$21.71	$16.35	$13.76	$12.29	$11.36
$3,000	$32.56	$24.52	$20.64	$18.43	$17.04
$4,000	$43.42	$32.69	$27.52	$24.57	$22.72
$5,000	$54.27	$40.86	$34.40	$30.71	$28.39
$6,000	$65.12	$49.03	$41.28	$36.85	$34.07
$7,000	$75.97	$57.20	$48.16	$42.99	$39.75
$8,000	$86.83	$65.37	$55.04	$49.13	$45.43
$9,000	$97.68	$73.54	$61.91	$55.27	$51.11
$10,000	$108.53	$81.71	$68.79	$61.41	$56.78
$15,000	$162.79	$122.57	$103.19	$92.12	$85.17
$20,000	$217.06	$163.42	$137.58	$122.82	$113.56
$25,000	$271.32	$204.28	$171.98	$153.53	$141.95
$30,000	$325.58	$245.13	$206.37	$184.23	$170.34
$35,000	$379.85	$285.98	$240.77	$214.94	$198.73
$40,000	$434.11	$326.84	$275.16	$245.64	$227.12
$45,000	$488.37	$367.69	$309.55	$276.34	$255.51
$50,000	$542.64	$408.55	$343.95	$307.05	$283.90
$55,000	$596.90	$449.40	$378.34	$337.75	$312.29
$60,000	$651.16	$490.26	$412.74	$368.46	$340.68
$65,000	$705.43	$531.11	$447.13	$399.16	$369.07
$70,000	$759.69	$571.96	$481.53	$429.87	$397.46
$75,000	$813.95	$612.82	$515.92	$460.57	$425.85
$80,000	$868.22	$653.67	$550.31	$491.27	$454.24
$85,000	$922.48	$694.53	$584.71	$521.98	$482.63
$90,000	$976.74	$735.38	$619.10	$552.68	$511.02
$95,000	$1,031.00	$776.23	$653.50	$583.39	$539.40
$100,000	$1,085.27	$817.09	$687.89	$614.09	$567.79
$110,000	$1,193.79	$898.80	$756.68	$675.50	$624.57
$120,000	$1,302.32	$980.51	$825.47	$736.91	$681.35
$125,000	$1,356.58	$1,021.36	$859.86	$767.61	$709.74
$130,000	$1,410.85	$1,062.21	$894.26	$798.32	$738.13
$140,000	$1,519.37	$1,143.92	$963.05	$859.73	$794.91
$150,000	$1,627.90	$1,225.63	$1,031.84	$921.14	$851.69
$160,000	$1,736.43	$1,307.34	$1,100.62	$982.54	$908.47
$170,000	$1,844.95	$1,389.05	$1,169.41	$1,043.95	$965.25
$175,000	$1,899.21	$1,429.90	$1,203.81	$1,074.66	$993.64
$180,000	$1,953.48	$1,470.76	$1,238.20	$1,105.36	$1,022.03
$190,000	$2,062.00	$1,552.46	$1,306.99	$1,166.77	$1,078.80
$200,000	$2,170.53	$1,634.17	$1,375.78	$1,228.18	$1,135.58
$210,000	$2,279.06	$1,715.88	$1,444.57	$1,289.59	$1,192.36
$220,000	$2,387.58	$1,797.59	$1,513.36	$1,351.00	$1,249.14
$225,000	$2,441.85	$1,838.44	$1,547.75	$1,381.70	$1,277.53
$230,000	$2,496.11	$1,879.30	$1,582.15	$1,412.41	$1,305.92
$240,000	$2,604.64	$1,961.01	$1,650.93	$1,473.81	$1,362.70
$250,000	$2,713.16	$2,042.71	$1,719.72	$1,535.22	$1,419.48
$260,000	$2,821.69	$2,124.42	$1,788.51	$1,596.63	$1,476.26
$270,000	$2,930.21	$2,206.13	$1,857.30	$1,658.04	$1,533.04
$275,000	$2,984.48	$2,246.98	$1,891.70	$1,688.75	$1,561.42
$280,000	$3,038.74	$2,287.84	$1,926.09	$1,719.45	$1,589.81
$290,000	$3,147.27	$2,369.55	$1,994.88	$1,780.86	$1,646.59
$300,000	$3,255.79	$2,451.26	$2,063.67	$1,842.27	$1,703.37

With an interest rate of 5.5%, your monthly payment will be:

Loan Amount	Number of Years in Term				
	10	15	20	25	30
$310,000	$3,364.32	$2,532.96	$2,132.46	$1,903.68	$1,760.15
$320,000	$3,472.85	$2,614.67	$2,201.24	$1,965.08	$1,816.93
$325,000	$3,527.11	$2,655.53	$2,235.64	$1,995.79	$1,845.32
$330,000	$3,581.37	$2,696.38	$2,270.03	$2,026.49	$1,873.71
$340,000	$3,689.90	$2,778.09	$2,338.82	$2,087.90	$1,930.49
$350,000	$3,798.42	$2,859.80	$2,407.61	$2,149.31	$1,987.27
$360,000	$3,906.95	$2,941.51	$2,476.40	$2,210.72	$2,044.05
$370,000	$4,015.48	$3,023.21	$2,545.19	$2,272.13	$2,100.82
$375,000	$4,069.74	$3,064.07	$2,579.58	$2,302.83	$2,129.21
$380,000	$4,124.00	$3,104.92	$2,613.98	$2,333.54	$2,157.60
$390,000	$4,232.53	$3,186.63	$2,682.77	$2,394.95	$2,214.38
$400,000	$4,341.06	$3,268.34	$2,751.55	$2,456.35	$2,271.16

With an interest rate of 5.75%, your monthly payment will be:

Loan Amount	Number of Years in Term				
	10	15	20	25	30
$1,000	$10.98	$8.31	$6.47	$5.71	$5.22
$2,000	$21.96	$16.61	$12.93	$11.41	$10.44
$3,000	$32.94	$24.92	$19.39	$17.11	$15.65
$4,000	$43.91	$33.22	$25.85	$22.81	$20.87
$5,000	$54.89	$41.53	$32.32	$28.51	$26.09
$6,000	$65.87	$49.83	$38.78	$34.21	$31.30
$7,000	$76.84	$58.13	$45.24	$39.91	$36.52
$8,000	$87.82	$66.44	$51.70	$45.61	$41.74
$9,000	$98.80	$74.74	$58.17	$51.32	$46.95
$10,000	$109.77	$83.05	$64.63	$57.02	$52.17
$15,000	$164.66	$124.57	$96.94	$85.52	$78.25
$20,000	$219.54	$166.09	$129.25	$114.03	$104.33
$25,000	$274.43	$207.61	$161.56	$142.53	$130.42
$30,000	$329.31	$249.13	$193.87	$171.04	$156.50
$35,000	$384.20	$290.65	$226.18	$199.55	$182.58
$40,000	$439.08	$332.17	$258.49	$228.05	$208.66
$45,000	$493.97	$373.69	$290.81	$256.56	$234.75
$50,000	$548.85	$415.21	$323.12	$285.06	$260.83
$55,000	$603.74	$456.73	$355.43	$313.57	$286.91
$60,000	$658.62	$498.25	$387.74	$342.08	$312.99
$65,000	$713.50	$539.77	$420.05	$370.58	$339.08
$70,000	$768.39	$581.29	$452.36	$399.09	$365.16
$75,000	$823.27	$622.81	$484.67	$427.59	$391.24
$80,000	$878.16	$664.33	$516.98	$456.10	$417.32
$85,000	$933.04	$705.85	$549.30	$484.60	$443.41
$90,000	$987.93	$747.37	$581.61	$513.11	$469.49
$95,000	$1,042.81	$788.89	$613.92	$541.62	$495.57
$100,000	$1,097.70	$830.42	$646.23	$570.12	$521.65
$110,000	$1,207.47	$913.46	$710.85	$627.13	$573.82
$120,000	$1,317.24	$996.50	$775.47	$684.15	$625.98
$125,000	$1,372.12	$1,038.02	$807.78	$712.65	$652.06
$130,000	$1,427.00	$1,079.54	$840.10	$741.16	$678.15
$140,000	$1,536.77	$1,162.58	$904.72	$798.17	$730.31
$150,000	$1,646.54	$1,245.62	$969.34	$855.18	$782.48

With an interest rate of 5.75%, your monthly payment will be:

Loan Amount	Number of Years in Term				
	10	15	20	25	30
$160,000	$1,756.31	$1,328.66	$1,123.34	$1,006.58	$933.72
$170,000	$1,866.08	$1,411.70	$1,193.55	$1,069.49	$992.08
$175,000	$1,920.97	$1,453.22	$1,228.65	$1,100.94	$1,021.26
$180,000	$1,975.85	$1,494.74	$1,263.76	$1,132.40	$1,050.44
$190,000	$2,085.62	$1,577.78	$1,333.96	$1,195.31	$1,108.79
$200,000	$2,195.39	$1,660.83	$1,404.17	$1,258.22	$1,167.15
$210,000	$2,305.16	$1,743.87	$1,474.38	$1,321.13	$1,225.51
$220,000	$2,414.93	$1,826.91	$1,544.59	$1,384.04	$1,283.87
$225,000	$2,469.81	$1,868.43	$1,579.69	$1,415.49	$1,313.04
$230,000	$2,524.70	$1,909.95	$1,614.80	$1,446.95	$1,342.22
$240,000	$2,634.47	$1,992.99	$1,685.01	$1,509.86	$1,400.58
$250,000	$2,744.24	$2,076.03	$1,755.21	$1,572.77	$1,458.94
$260,000	$2,854.00	$2,159.07	$1,825.42	$1,635.68	$1,517.29
$270,000	$2,963.77	$2,242.11	$1,895.63	$1,698.59	$1,575.65
$275,000	$3,018.66	$2,283.63	$1,930.73	$1,730.05	$1,604.83
$280,000	$3,073.54	$2,325.15	$1,965.84	$1,761.50	$1,634.01
$290,000	$3,183.31	$2,408.19	$2,036.05	$1,824.41	$1,692.37
$300,000	$3,293.08	$2,491.24	$2,106.26	$1,887.32	$1,750.72
$310,000	$3,402.85	$2,574.28	$2,176.46	$1,950.23	$1,809.08
$320,000	$3,512.62	$2,657.32	$2,246.67	$2,013.15	$1,867.44
$325,000	$3,567.50	$2,698.84	$2,281.78	$2,044.60	$1,896.62
$330,000	$3,622.39	$2,740.36	$2,316.88	$2,076.06	$1,925.80
$340,000	$3,732.16	$2,823.40	$2,387.09	$2,138.97	$1,984.15
$350,000	$3,841.93	$2,906.44	$2,457.30	$2,201.88	$2,042.51
$360,000	$3,951.70	$2,989.48	$2,527.51	$2,264.79	$2,100.87
$370,000	$4,061.47	$3,072.52	$2,597.71	$2,327.70	$2,159.22
$375,000	$4,116.35	$3,114.04	$2,632.82	$2,359.15	$2,188.40
$380,000	$4,171.24	$3,155.56	$2,667.92	$2,390.61	$2,217.58
$390,000	$4,281.00	$3,238.60	$2,738.13	$2,453.52	$2,275.94
$400,000	$4,390.77	$3,321.65	$2,808.34	$2,516.43	$2,334.30

With an interest rate of 6.00%, your monthly payment will be:

Loan Amount	Number of Years in Term				
	10	15	20	25	30
$1,000	$11.11	$8.44	$7.17	$6.45	$6.00
$2,000	$22.21	$16.88	$14.33	$12.89	$12.00
$3,000	$33.31	$25.32	$21.50	$19.33	$17.99
$4,000	$44.41	$33.76	$28.66	$25.78	$23.99
$5,000	$55.52	$42.20	$35.83	$32.22	$29.98
$6,000	$66.62	$50.64	$42.99	$38.66	$35.98
$7,000	$77.72	$59.07	$50.16	$45.11	$41.97
$8,000	$88.82	$67.51	$57.32	$51.55	$47.97
$9,000	$99.92	$75.95	$64.48	$57.99	$53.96
$10,000	$111.03	$84.39	$71.65	$64.44	$59.96
$15,000	$166.54	$126.58	$107.47	$96.65	$89.94
$20,000	$222.05	$168.78	$143.29	$128.87	$119.92
$25,000	$277.56	$210.97	$179.11	$161.08	$149.89
$30,000	$333.07	$253.16	$214.93	$193.30	$179.87

With an interest rate of 6.00%, your monthly payment will be:

Loan Amount	Number of Years in Term				
	10	15	20	25	30
$35,000	$388.58	$295.35	$250.76	$225.51	$209.85
$40,000	$444.09	$337.55	$286.58	$257.73	$239.83
$45,000	$499.60	$379.74	$322.40	$289.94	$269.80
$50,000	$555.11	$421.93	$358.22	$322.16	$299.78
$55,000	$610.62	$464.13	$394.04	$354.37	$329.76
$60,000	$666.13	$506.32	$429.86	$386.59	$359.74
$65,000	$721.64	$548.51	$465.69	$418.80	$389.71
$70,000	$777.15	$590.70	$501.51	$451.02	$419.69
$75,000	$832.66	$632.90	$537.33	$483.23	$449.67
$80,000	$888.17	$675.09	$573.15	$515.45	$479.65
$85,000	$943.68	$717.28	$608.97	$547.66	$509.62
$90,000	$999.19	$759.48	$644.79	$579.88	$539.60
$95,000	$1,054.70	$801.67	$680.61	$612.09	$569.58
$100,000	$1,110.21	$843.86	$716.44	$644.31	$599.56
$110,000	$1,221.23	$928.25	$788.08	$708.74	$659.51
$120,000	$1,332.25	$1,012.63	$859.72	$773.17	$719.47
$125,000	$1,387.76	$1,054.83	$895.54	$805.38	$749.44
$130,000	$1,443.27	$1,097.02	$931.37	$837.60	$779.42
$140,000	$1,554.29	$1,181.40	$1,003.01	$902.03	$839.38
$150,000	$1,665.31	$1,265.79	$1,074.65	$966.46	$899.33
$160,000	$1,776.33	$1,350.18	$1,146.29	$1,030.89	$959.29
$170,000	$1,887.35	$1,434.56	$1,217.94	$1,095.32	$1,019.24
$175,000	$1,942.86	$1,476.75	$1,253.76	$1,127.53	$1,049.22
$180,000	$1,998.37	$1,518.95	$1,289.58	$1,159.75	$1,079.20
$190,000	$2,109.39	$1,603.33	$1,361.22	$1,224.18	$1,139.15
$200,000	$2,220.42	$1,687.72	$1,432.87	$1,288.61	$1,199.11
$210,000	$2,331.44	$1,772.10	$1,504.51	$1,353.04	$1,259.06
$220,000	$2,442.46	$1,856.49	$1,576.15	$1,417.47	$1,319.02
$225,000	$2,497.97	$1,898.68	$1,611.97	$1,449.68	$1,348.99
$230,000	$2,553.48	$1,940.88	$1,647.80	$1,481.90	$1,378.97
$240,000	$2,664.50	$2,025.26	$1,719.44	$1,546.33	$1,438.93
$250,000	$2,775.52	$2,109.65	$1,791.08	$1,610.76	$1,498.88
$260,000	$2,886.54	$2,194.03	$1,862.73	$1,675.19	$1,558.84
$270,000	$2,997.56	$2,278.42	$1,934.37	$1,739.62	$1,618.79
$275,000	$3,053.07	$2,320.61	$1,970.19	$1,771.83	$1,648.77
$280,000	$3,108.58	$2,362.80	$2,006.01	$1,804.05	$1,678.75
$290,000	$3,219.60	$2,447.19	$2,077.66	$1,868.48	$1,738.70
$300,000	$3,330.62	$2,531.58	$2,149.30	$1,932.91	$1,798.66
$310,000	$3,441.64	$2,615.96	$2,220.94	$1,997.34	$1,858.61
$320,000	$3,552.66	$2,700.35	$2,292.58	$2,061.77	$1,918.57
$325,000	$3,608.17	$2,742.54	$2,328.41	$2,093.98	$1,948.54
$330,000	$3,663.68	$2,784.73	$2,364.23	$2,126.20	$1,978.52
$340,000	$3,774.70	$2,869.12	$2,435.87	$2,190.63	$2,038.48
$350,000	$3,885.72	$2,953.50	$2,507.51	$2,255.06	$2,098.43
$360,000	$3,996.74	$3,037.89	$2,579.16	$2,319.49	$2,158.39
$370,000	$4,107.76	$3,122.28	$2,650.80	$2,383.92	$2,218.34
$375,000	$4,163.27	$3,164.47	$2,686.62	$2,416.14	$2,248.32
$380,000	$4,218.78	$3,206.66	$2,722.44	$2,448.35	$2,278.30
$390,000	$4,329.80	$3,291.05	$2,794.09	$2,512.78	$2,338.25
$400,000	$4,440.83	$3,375.43	$2,865.73	$2,577.21	$2,398.21

With an interest rate of 6.25%, your monthly payment will be:

Loan Amount	Number of Years in Term				
	10	15	20	25	30
$1,000	$11.23	$8.58	$7.31	$6.60	$6.16
$2,000	$22.46	$17.15	$14.62	$13.20	$12.32
$3,000	$33.69	$25.73	$21.93	$19.80	$18.48
$4,000	$44.92	$34.30	$29.24	$26.39	$24.63
$5,000	$56.15	$42.88	$36.55	$32.99	$30.79
$6,000	$67.37	$51.45	$43.86	$39.59	$36.95
$7,000	$78.60	$60.02	$51.17	$46.18	$43.11
$8,000	$89.83	$68.60	$58.48	$52.78	$49.26
$9,000	$101.06	$77.17	$65.79	$59.38	$55.42
$10,000	$112.29	$85.75	$73.10	$65.97	$61.58
$15,000	$168.43	$128.62	$109.64	$98.96	$92.36
$20,000	$224.57	$171.49	$146.19	$131.94	$123.15
$25,000	$280.71	$214.36	$182.74	$164.92	$153.93
$30,000	$336.85	$257.23	$219.28	$197.91	$184.72
$35,000	$392.99	$300.10	$255.83	$230.89	$215.51
$40,000	$449.13	$342.97	$292.38	$263.87	$246.29
$45,000	$505.27	$385.85	$328.92	$296.86	$277.08
$50,000	$561.41	$428.72	$365.47	$329.84	$307.86
$55,000	$617.55	$471.59	$402.02	$362.82	$338.65
$60,000	$673.69	$514.46	$438.56	$395.81	$369.44
$65,000	$729.83	$557.33	$475.11	$428.79	$400.22
$70,000	$785.97	$600.20	$511.65	$461.77	$431.01
$75,000	$842.11	$643.07	$548.20	$494.76	$461.79
$80,000	$898.25	$685.94	$584.75	$527.74	$492.58
$85,000	$954.39	$728.81	$621.29	$560.72	$523.36
$90,000	$1,010.53	$771.69	$657.84	$593.71	$554.15
$95,000	$1,066.67	$814.56	$694.39	$626.69	$584.94
$100,000	$1,122.81	$857.43	$730.93	$659.67	$615.72
$110,000	$1,235.09	$943.17	$804.03	$725.64	$677.29
$120,000	$1,347.37	$1,028.91	$877.12	$791.61	$738.87
$125,000	$1,403.51	$1,071.78	$913.67	$824.59	$769.65
$130,000	$1,459.65	$1,114.65	$950.21	$857.58	$800.44
$140,000	$1,571.93	$1,200.40	$1,023.30	$923.54	$862.01
$150,000	$1,684.21	$1,286.14	$1,096.40	$989.51	$923.58
$160,000	$1,796.49	$1,371.88	$1,169.49	$1,055.48	$985.15
$170,000	$1,908.77	$1,457.62	$1,242.58	$1,121.44	$1,046.72
$175,000	$1,964.91	$1,500.50	$1,279.13	$1,154.43	$1,077.51
$180,000	$2,021.05	$1,543.37	$1,315.68	$1,187.41	$1,108.30
$190,000	$2,133.33	$1,629.11	$1,388.77	$1,253.38	$1,169.87
$200,000	$2,245.61	$1,714.85	$1,461.86	$1,319.34	$1,231.44
$210,000	$2,357.89	$1,800.59	$1,534.95	$1,385.31	$1,293.01
$220,000	$2,470.17	$1,886.34	$1,608.05	$1,451.28	$1,354.58
$225,000	$2,526.31	$1,929.21	$1,644.59	$1,484.26	$1,385.37
$230,000	$2,582.45	$1,972.08	$1,681.14	$1,517.24	$1,416.15
$240,000	$2,694.73	$2,057.82	$1,754.23	$1,583.21	$1,477.73
$250,000	$2,807.01	$2,143.56	$1,827.33	$1,649.18	$1,539.30
$260,000	$2,919.29	$2,229.30	$1,900.42	$1,715.15	$1,600.87
$270,000	$3,031.57	$2,315.05	$1,973.51	$1,781.11	$1,662.44
$275,000	$3,087.71	$2,357.92	$2,010.06	$1,814.10	$1,693.23
$280,000	$3,143.85	$2,400.79	$2,046.60	$1,847.08	$1,724.01
$290,000	$3,256.13	$2,486.53	$2,119.70	$1,913.05	$1,785.58
$300,000	$3,368.41	$2,572.27	$2,192.79	$1,979.01	$1,847.16

With an interest rate of 6.25%, your monthly payment will be:

Loan Amount	Number of Years in Term				
	10	15	20	25	30
$310,000	$3,480.69	$2,658.02	$2,265.88	$2,044.98	$1,908.73
$320,000	$3,592.97	$2,743.76	$2,338.98	$2,110.95	$1,970.30
$325,000	$3,649.11	$2,786.63	$2,375.52	$2,143.93	$2,001.09
$330,000	$3,705.25	$2,829.50	$2,412.07	$2,176.91	$2,031.87
$340,000	$3,817.53	$2,915.24	$2,485.16	$2,242.88	$2,093.44
$350,000	$3,929.81	$3,000.99	$2,558.25	$2,308.85	$2,155.02
$360,000	$4,042.09	$3,086.73	$2,631.35	$2,374.81	$2,216.59
$370,000	$4,154.37	$3,172.47	$2,704.44	$2,440.78	$2,278.16
$375,000	$4,210.51	$3,215.34	$2,740.99	$2,473.77	$2,308.94
$380,000	$4,266.65	$3,258.21	$2,777.53	$2,506.75	$2,339.73
$390,000	$4,378.93	$3,343.95	$2,850.62	$2,572.72	$2,401.30
$400,000	$4,491.21	$3,429.70	$2,923.72	$2,638.68	$2,462.87

With an interest rate of 6.5%, your monthly payment will be:

Loan Amount	Number of Years in Term				
	10	15	20	25	30
$1,000	$11.36	$8.72	$7.46	$6.76	$6.33
$2,000	$22.71	$17.43	$14.92	$13.51	$12.65
$3,000	$34.07	$26.14	$22.37	$20.26	$18.97
$4,000	$45.42	$34.85	$29.83	$27.01	$25.29
$5,000	$56.78	$43.56	$37.28	$33.77	$31.61
$6,000	$68.13	$52.27	$44.74	$40.52	$37.93
$7,000	$79.49	$60.98	$52.20	$47.27	$44.25
$8,000	$90.84	$69.69	$59.65	$54.02	$50.57
$9,000	$102.20	$78.40	$67.11	$60.77	$56.89
$10,000	$113.55	$87.12	$74.56	$67.53	$63.21
$15,000	$170.33	$130.67	$111.84	$101.29	$94.82
$20,000	$227.10	$174.23	$149.12	$135.05	$126.42
$25,000	$283.87	$217.78	$186.40	$168.81	$158.02
$30,000	$340.65	$261.34	$223.68	$202.57	$189.63
$35,000	$397.42	$304.89	$260.96	$236.33	$221.23
$40,000	$454.20	$348.45	$298.23	$270.09	$252.83
$45,000	$510.97	$392.00	$335.51	$303.85	$284.44
$50,000	$567.74	$435.56	$372.79	$337.61	$316.04
$55,000	$624.52	$479.11	$410.07	$371.37	$347.64
$60,000	$681.29	$522.67	$447.35	$405.13	$379.25
$65,000	$738.07	$566.22	$484.63	$438.89	$410.85
$70,000	$794.84	$609.78	$521.91	$472.65	$442.45
$75,000	$851.61	$653.34	$559.18	$506.41	$474.06
$80,000	$908.39	$696.89	$596.46	$540.17	$505.66
$85,000	$965.16	$740.45	$633.74	$573.93	$537.26
$90,000	$1,021.94	$784.00	$671.02	$607.69	$568.87
$95,000	$1,078.71	$827.56	$708.30	$641.45	$600.47
$100,000	$1,135.48	$871.11	$745.58	$675.21	$632.07
$110,000	$1,249.03	$958.22	$820.14	$742.73	$695.28
$120,000	$1,362.58	$1,045.33	$894.69	$810.25	$758.49
$125,000	$1,419.35	$1,088.89	$931.97	$844.01	$790.09
$130,000	$1,476.13	$1,132.44	$969.25	$877.77	$821.69
$140,000	$1,589.68	$1,219.56	$1,043.81	$945.30	$884.90
$150,000	$1,703.22	$1,306.67	$1,118.36	$1,012.82	$948.11

With an interest rate of 6.5%, your monthly payment will be:

Loan Amount	Number of Years in Term				
	10	15	20	25	30
$160,000	$1,816.77	$1,393.78	$1,192.92	$1,080.34	$1,011.31
$170,000	$1,930.32	$1,480.89	$1,267.48	$1,147.86	$1,074.52
$175,000	$1,987.09	$1,524.44	$1,304.76	$1,181.62	$1,106.12
$180,000	$2,043.87	$1,568.00	$1,342.04	$1,215.38	$1,137.73
$190,000	$2,157.42	$1,655.11	$1,416.59	$1,282.90	$1,200.93
$200,000	$2,270.96	$1,742.22	$1,491.15	$1,350.42	$1,264.14
$210,000	$2,384.51	$1,829.33	$1,565.71	$1,417.94	$1,327.35
$220,000	$2,498.06	$1,916.44	$1,640.27	$1,485.46	$1,390.55
$225,000	$2,554.83	$1,960.00	$1,677.54	$1,519.22	$1,422.16
$230,000	$2,611.61	$2,003.55	$1,714.82	$1,552.98	$1,453.76
$240,000	$2,725.16	$2,090.66	$1,789.38	$1,620.50	$1,516.97
$250,000	$2,838.70	$2,177.77	$1,863.94	$1,688.02	$1,580.18
$260,000	$2,952.25	$2,264.88	$1,938.50	$1,755.54	$1,643.38
$270,000	$3,065.80	$2,351.99	$2,013.05	$1,823.06	$1,706.59
$275,000	$3,122.57	$2,395.55	$2,050.33	$1,856.82	$1,738.19
$280,000	$3,179.35	$2,439.11	$2,087.61	$1,890.59	$1,769.80
$290,000	$3,292.90	$2,526.22	$2,162.17	$1,958.11	$1,833.00
$300,000	$3,406.44	$2,613.33	$2,236.72	$2,025.63	$1,896.21
$310,000	$3,519.99	$2,700.44	$2,311.28	$2,093.15	$1,959.42
$320,000	$3,633.54	$2,787.55	$2,385.84	$2,160.67	$2,022.62
$325,000	$3,690.31	$2,831.10	$2,423.12	$2,194.43	$2,054.23
$330,000	$3,747.09	$2,874.66	$2,460.40	$2,228.19	$2,085.83
$340,000	$3,860.64	$2,961.77	$2,534.95	$2,295.71	$2,149.04
$350,000	$3,974.18	$3,048.88	$2,609.51	$2,363.23	$2,212.24
$360,000	$4,087.73	$3,135.99	$2,684.07	$2,430.75	$2,275.45
$370,000	$4,201.28	$3,223.10	$2,758.63	$2,498.27	$2,338.66
$375,000	$4,258.05	$3,266.66	$2,795.90	$2,532.03	$2,370.26
$380,000	$4,314.83	$3,310.21	$2,833.18	$2,565.79	$2,401.86
$390,000	$4,428.38	$3,397.32	$2,907.74	$2,633.31	$2,465.07
$400,000	$4,541.92	$3,484.43	$2,982.30	$2,700.83	$2,528.28

With an interest rate of 6.75%, your monthly payment will be:

Loan Amount	Number of Years in Term				
	10	15	20	25	30
$1,000	$11.49	$8.85	$7.61	$6.91	$6.49
$2,000	$22.97	$17.70	$15.21	$13.82	$12.98
$3,000	$34.45	$26.55	$22.82	$20.73	$19.46
$4,000	$45.93	$35.40	$30.42	$27.64	$25.95
$5,000	$57.42	$44.25	$38.02	$34.55	$32.43
$6,000	$68.90	$53.10	$45.63	$41.46	$38.92
$7,000	$80.38	$61.95	$53.23	$48.37	$45.41
$8,000	$91.86	$70.80	$60.83	$55.28	$51.89
$9,000	$103.35	$79.65	$68.44	$62.19	$58.38
$10,000	$114.83	$88.50	$76.04	$69.10	$64.86
$15,000	$172.24	$132.74	$114.06	$103.64	$97.29
$20,000	$229.65	$176.99	$152.08	$138.19	$129.72
$25,000	$287.07	$221.23	$190.10	$172.73	$162.15
$30,000	$344.48	$265.48	$228.11	$207.28	$194.58

With an interest rate of 6.75%, your monthly payment will be:

Loan Amount	Number of Years in Term				
	10	15	20	25	30
$35,000	$401.89	$309.72	$266.13	$241.82	$227.01
$40,000	$459.30	$353.97	$304.15	$276.37	$259.44
$45,000	$516.71	$398.21	$342.17	$310.92	$291.87
$50,000	$574.13	$442.46	$380.19	$345.46	$324.30
$55,000	$631.54	$486.71	$418.21	$380.01	$356.73
$60,000	$688.95	$530.95	$456.22	$414.55	$389.16
$65,000	$746.36	$575.20	$494.24	$449.10	$421.59
$70,000	$803.77	$619.44	$532.26	$483.64	$454.02
$75,000	$861.19	$663.69	$570.28	$518.19	$486.45
$80,000	$918.60	$707.93	$608.30	$552.73	$518.88
$85,000	$976.01	$752.18	$646.31	$587.28	$551.31
$90,000	$1,033.42	$796.42	$684.33	$621.83	$583.74
$95,000	$1,090.83	$840.67	$722.35	$656.37	$616.17
$100,000	$1,148.25	$884.91	$760.37	$690.92	$648.60
$110,000	$1,263.07	$973.41	$836.41	$760.01	$713.46
$120,000	$1,377.89	$1,061.90	$912.44	$829.10	$778.32
$125,000	$1,435.31	$1,106.14	$950.46	$863.64	$810.75
$130,000	$1,492.72	$1,150.39	$988.48	$898.19	$843.18
$140,000	$1,607.54	$1,238.88	$1,064.51	$967.28	$908.04
$150,000	$1,722.37	$1,327.37	$1,140.55	$1,036.37	$972.90
$160,000	$1,837.19	$1,415.86	$1,216.59	$1,105.46	$1,037.76
$170,000	$1,952.01	$1,504.35	$1,292.62	$1,174.55	$1,102.62
$175,000	$2,009.43	$1,548.60	$1,330.64	$1,209.10	$1,135.05
$180,000	$2,066.84	$1,592.84	$1,368.66	$1,243.65	$1,167.48
$190,000	$2,181.66	$1,681.33	$1,444.70	$1,312.74	$1,232.34
$200,000	$2,296.49	$1,769.82	$1,520.73	$1,381.83	$1,297.20
$210,000	$2,411.31	$1,858.31	$1,596.77	$1,450.92	$1,362.06
$220,000	$2,526.14	$1,946.81	$1,672.81	$1,520.01	$1,426.92
$225,000	$2,583.55	$1,991.05	$1,710.82	$1,554.56	$1,459.35
$230,000	$2,640.96	$2,035.30	$1,748.84	$1,589.10	$1,491.78
$240,000	$2,755.78	$2,123.79	$1,824.88	$1,658.19	$1,556.64
$250,000	$2,870.61	$2,212.28	$1,900.92	$1,727.28	$1,621.50
$260,000	$2,985.43	$2,300.77	$1,976.95	$1,796.37	$1,686.36
$270,000	$3,100.26	$2,389.26	$2,052.99	$1,865.47	$1,751.22
$275,000	$3,157.67	$2,433.51	$2,091.01	$1,900.01	$1,783.65
$280,000	$3,215.08	$2,477.75	$2,129.02	$1,934.56	$1,816.08
$290,000	$3,329.90	$2,566.24	$2,205.06	$2,003.65	$1,880.94
$300,000	$3,444.73	$2,654.73	$2,281.10	$2,072.74	$1,945.80
$310,000	$3,559.55	$2,743.22	$2,357.13	$2,141.83	$2,010.66
$320,000	$3,674.38	$2,831.72	$2,433.17	$2,210.92	$2,075.52
$325,000	$3,731.79	$2,875.96	$2,471.19	$2,245.47	$2,107.95
$330,000	$3,789.20	$2,920.21	$2,509.21	$2,280.01	$2,140.38
$340,000	$3,904.02	$3,008.70	$2,585.24	$2,349.10	$2,205.24
$350,000	$4,018.85	$3,097.19	$2,661.28	$2,418.20	$2,270.10
$360,000	$4,133.67	$3,185.68	$2,737.32	$2,487.29	$2,334.96
$370,000	$4,248.50	$3,274.17	$2,813.35	$2,556.38	$2,399.82
$375,000	$4,305.91	$3,318.42	$2,851.37	$2,590.92	$2,432.25
$380,000	$4,363.32	$3,362.66	$2,889.39	$2,625.47	$2,464.68
$390,000	$4,478.15	$3,451.15	$2,965.42	$2,694.56	$2,529.54
$400,000	$4,592.97	$3,539.64	$3,041.46	$2,763.65	$2,594.40

With an interest rate of 7.00%, your monthly payment will be:

Loan Amount	Number of Years in Term				
	10	15	20	25	30
$1,000	$11.62	$8.99	$7.76	$7.07	$6.66
$2,000	$23.23	$17.98	$15.51	$14.14	$13.31
$3,000	$34.84	$26.97	$23.26	$21.21	$19.96
$4,000	$46.45	$35.96	$31.02	$28.28	$26.62
$5,000	$58.06	$44.95	$38.77	$35.34	$33.27
$6,000	$69.67	$53.93	$46.52	$42.41	$39.92
$7,000	$81.28	$62.92	$54.28	$49.48	$46.58
$8,000	$92.89	$71.91	$62.03	$56.55	$53.23
$9,000	$104.50	$80.90	$69.78	$63.62	$59.88
$10,000	$116.11	$89.89	$77.53	$70.68	$66.54
$15,000	$174.17	$134.83	$116.30	$106.02	$99.80
$20,000	$232.22	$179.77	$155.06	$141.36	$133.07
$25,000	$290.28	$224.71	$193.83	$176.70	$166.33
$30,000	$348.33	$269.65	$232.59	$212.04	$199.60
$35,000	$406.38	$314.59	$271.36	$247.38	$232.86
$40,000	$464.44	$359.54	$310.12	$282.72	$266.13
$45,000	$522.49	$404.48	$348.89	$318.06	$299.39
$50,000	$580.55	$449.42	$387.65	$353.39	$332.66
$55,000	$638.60	$494.36	$426.42	$388.73	$365.92
$60,000	$696.66	$539.30	$465.18	$424.07	$399.19
$65,000	$754.71	$584.24	$503.95	$459.41	$432.45
$70,000	$812.76	$629.18	$542.71	$494.75	$465.72
$75,000	$870.82	$674.13	$581.48	$530.09	$498.98
$80,000	$928.87	$719.07	$620.24	$565.43	$532.25
$85,000	$986.93	$764.01	$659.01	$600.77	$565.51
$90,000	$1,044.98	$808.95	$697.77	$636.11	$598.78
$95,000	$1,103.04	$853.89	$736.54	$671.45	$632.04
$100,000	$1,161.09	$898.83	$775.30	$706.78	$665.31
$110,000	$1,277.20	$988.72	$852.83	$777.46	$731.84
$120,000	$1,393.31	$1,078.60	$930.36	$848.14	$798.37
$125,000	$1,451.36	$1,123.54	$969.13	$883.48	$831.63
$130,000	$1,509.42	$1,168.48	$1,007.89	$918.82	$864.90
$140,000	$1,625.52	$1,258.36	$1,085.42	$989.50	$931.43
$150,000	$1,741.63	$1,348.25	$1,162.95	$1,060.17	$997.96
$160,000	$1,857.74	$1,438.13	$1,240.48	$1,130.85	$1,064.49
$170,000	$1,973.85	$1,528.01	$1,318.01	$1,201.53	$1,131.02
$175,000	$2,031.90	$1,572.95	$1,356.78	$1,236.87	$1,164.28
$180,000	$2,089.96	$1,617.90	$1,395.54	$1,272.21	$1,197.55
$190,000	$2,206.07	$1,707.78	$1,473.07	$1,342.89	$1,264.08
$200,000	$2,322.17	$1,797.66	$1,550.60	$1,413.56	$1,330.61
$210,000	$2,438.28	$1,887.54	$1,628.13	$1,484.24	$1,397.14
$220,000	$2,554.39	$1,977.43	$1,705.66	$1,554.92	$1,463.67
$225,000	$2,612.45	$2,022.37	$1,744.43	$1,590.26	$1,496.94
$230,000	$2,670.50	$2,067.31	$1,783.19	$1,625.60	$1,530.20
$240,000	$2,786.61	$2,157.19	$1,860.72	$1,696.28	$1,596.73
$250,000	$2,902.72	$2,247.08	$1,938.25	$1,766.95	$1,663.26
$260,000	$3,018.83	$2,336.96	$2,015.78	$1,837.63	$1,729.79
$270,000	$3,134.93	$2,426.84	$2,093.31	$1,908.31	$1,796.32
$275,000	$3,192.99	$2,471.78	$2,132.08	$1,943.65	$1,829.59
$280,000	$3,251.04	$2,516.72	$2,170.84	$1,978.99	$1,862.85
$290,000	$3,367.15	$2,606.61	$2,248.37	$2,049.66	$1,929.38
$300,000	$3,483.26	$2,696.49	$2,325.90	$2,120.34	$1,995.91

With an interest rate of 7.00%, your monthly payment will be:

Loan Amount	Number of Years in Term				
	10	15	20	25	30
$310,000	$3,599.37	$2,786.37	$2,403.43	$2,191.02	$2,062.44
$320,000	$3,715.48	$2,876.26	$2,480.96	$2,261.70	$2,128.97
$325,000	$3,773.53	$2,921.20	$2,519.73	$2,297.04	$2,162.24
$330,000	$3,831.58	$2,966.14	$2,558.49	$2,332.38	$2,195.50
$340,000	$3,947.69	$3,056.02	$2,636.02	$2,403.05	$2,262.03
$350,000	$4,063.80	$3,145.90	$2,713.55	$2,473.73	$2,328.56
$360,000	$4,179.91	$3,235.79	$2,791.08	$2,544.41	$2,395.09
$370,000	$4,296.02	$3,325.67	$2,868.61	$2,615.09	$2,461.62
$375,000	$4,354.07	$3,370.61	$2,907.38	$2,650.43	$2,494.89
$380,000	$4,412.13	$3,415.55	$2,946.14	$2,685.77	$2,528.15
$390,000	$4,528.24	$3,505.44	$3,023.67	$2,756.44	$2,594.68
$400,000	$4,644.34	$3,595.32	$3,101.20	$2,827.12	$2,661.21

With an interest rate of 7.25%, your monthly payment will be:

Loan Amount	Number of Years in Term				
	10	15	20	25	30
$1,000	$11.75	$9.13	$7.91	$7.23	$6.83
$2,000	$23.49	$18.26	$15.81	$14.46	$13.65
$3,000	$35.23	$27.39	$23.72	$21.69	$20.47
$4,000	$46.97	$36.52	$31.62	$28.92	$27.29
$5,000	$58.71	$45.65	$39.52	$36.15	$34.11
$6,000	$70.45	$54.78	$47.43	$43.37	$40.94
$7,000	$82.19	$63.91	$55.33	$50.60	$47.76
$8,000	$93.93	$73.03	$63.24	$57.83	$54.58
$9,000	$105.67	$82.16	$71.14	$65.06	$61.40
$10,000	$117.41	$91.29	$79.04	$72.29	$68.22
$15,000	$176.11	$136.93	$118.56	$108.43	$102.33
$20,000	$234.81	$182.58	$158.08	$144.57	$136.44
$25,000	$293.51	$228.22	$197.60	$180.71	$170.55
$30,000	$352.21	$273.86	$237.12	$216.85	$204.66
$35,000	$410.91	$319.51	$276.64	$252.99	$238.77
$40,000	$469.61	$365.15	$316.16	$289.13	$272.88
$45,000	$528.31	$410.79	$355.67	$325.27	$306.98
$50,000	$587.01	$456.44	$395.19	$361.41	$341.09
$55,000	$645.71	$502.08	$434.71	$397.55	$375.20
$60,000	$704.41	$547.72	$474.23	$433.69	$409.31
$65,000	$763.11	$593.37	$513.75	$469.83	$443.42
$70,000	$821.81	$639.01	$553.27	$505.97	$477.53
$75,000	$880.51	$684.65	$592.79	$542.11	$511.64
$80,000	$939.21	$730.30	$632.31	$578.25	$545.75
$85,000	$997.91	$775.94	$671.82	$614.39	$579.85
$90,000	$1,056.61	$821.58	$711.34	$650.53	$613.96
$95,000	$1,115.31	$867.22	$750.86	$686.67	$648.07
$100,000	$1,174.02	$912.87	$790.38	$722.81	$682.18
$110,000	$1,291.42	$1,004.15	$869.42	$795.09	$750.40
$120,000	$1,408.82	$1,095.44	$948.46	$867.37	$818.62
$125,000	$1,467.52	$1,141.08	$987.97	$903.51	$852.73
$130,000	$1,526.22	$1,186.73	$1,027.49	$939.65	$886.83
$140,000	$1,643.62	$1,278.01	$1,106.53	$1,011.93	$955.05
$150,000	$1,761.02	$1,369.30	$1,185.57	$1,084.22	$1,023.27

With an interest rate of 7.25%, your monthly payment will be:

Loan Amount	Number of Years in Term				
	10	15	20	25	30
$160,000	$1,878.42	$1,460.59	$1,264.61	$1,156.50	$1,091.49
$170,000	$1,995.82	$1,551.87	$1,343.64	$1,228.78	$1,159.70
$175,000	$2,054.52	$1,597.52	$1,383.16	$1,264.92	$1,193.81
$180,000	$2,113.22	$1,643.16	$1,422.68	$1,301.06	$1,227.92
$190,000	$2,230.62	$1,734.44	$1,501.72	$1,373.34	$1,296.14
$200,000	$2,348.03	$1,825.73	$1,580.76	$1,445.62	$1,364.36
$210,000	$2,465.43	$1,917.02	$1,659.79	$1,517.90	$1,432.58
$220,000	$2,582.83	$2,008.30	$1,738.83	$1,590.18	$1,500.79
$225,000	$2,641.53	$2,053.95	$1,778.35	$1,626.32	$1,534.90
$230,000	$2,700.23	$2,099.59	$1,817.87	$1,662.46	$1,569.01
$240,000	$2,817.63	$2,190.88	$1,896.91	$1,734.74	$1,637.23
$250,000	$2,935.03	$2,282.16	$1,975.94	$1,807.02	$1,705.45
$260,000	$3,052.43	$2,373.45	$2,054.98	$1,879.30	$1,773.66
$270,000	$3,169.83	$2,464.73	$2,134.02	$1,951.58	$1,841.88
$275,000	$3,228.53	$2,510.38	$2,173.54	$1,987.72	$1,875.99
$280,000	$3,287.23	$2,556.02	$2,213.06	$2,023.86	$1,910.10
$290,000	$3,404.64	$2,647.31	$2,292.10	$2,096.14	$1,978.32
$300,000	$3,522.04	$2,738.59	$2,371.13	$2,168.43	$2,046.53
$310,000	$3,639.44	$2,829.88	$2,450.17	$2,240.71	$2,114.75
$320,000	$3,756.84	$2,921.17	$2,529.21	$2,312.99	$2,182.97
$325,000	$3,815.54	$2,966.81	$2,568.73	$2,349.13	$2,217.08
$330,000	$3,874.24	$3,012.45	$2,608.25	$2,385.27	$2,251.19
$340,000	$3,991.64	$3,103.74	$2,687.28	$2,457.55	$2,319.40
$350,000	$4,109.04	$3,195.03	$2,766.32	$2,529.83	$2,387.62
$360,000	$4,226.44	$3,286.31	$2,845.36	$2,602.11	$2,455.84
$370,000	$4,343.84	$3,377.60	$2,924.40	$2,674.39	$2,524.06
$375,000	$4,402.54	$3,423.24	$2,963.91	$2,710.53	$2,558.17
$380,000	$4,461.24	$3,468.88	$3,003.43	$2,746.67	$2,592.27
$390,000	$4,578.65	$3,560.17	$3,082.47	$2,818.95	$2,660.49
$400,000	$4,696.05	$3,651.46	$3,161.51	$2,891.23	$2,728.71

With an interest rate of 7.5%, your monthly payment will be:

Loan Amount	Number of Years in Term				
	10	15	20	25	30
$1,000	$11.88	$9.28	$8.06	$7.39	$7.00
$2,000	$23.75	$18.55	$16.12	$14.78	$13.99
$3,000	$35.62	$27.82	$24.17	$22.17	$20.98
$4,000	$47.49	$37.09	$32.23	$29.56	$27.97
$5,000	$59.36	$46.36	$40.28	$36.95	$34.97
$6,000	$71.23	$55.63	$48.34	$44.34	$41.96
$7,000	$83.10	$64.90	$56.40	$51.73	$48.95
$8,000	$94.97	$74.17	$64.45	$59.12	$55.94
$9,000	$106.84	$83.44	$72.51	$66.51	$62.93
$10,000	$118.71	$92.71	$80.56	$73.90	$69.93
$15,000	$178.06	$139.06	$120.84	$110.85	$104.89
$20,000	$237.41	$185.41	$161.12	$147.80	$139.85
$25,000	$296.76	$231.76	$201.40	$184.75	$174.81
$30,000	$356.11	$278.11	$241.68	$221.70	$209.77

With an interest rate of 7.5%, your monthly payment will be:

Loan Amount	Number of Years in Term				
	10	15	20	25	30
$35,000	$415.46	$324.46	$281.96	$258.65	$244.73
$40,000	$474.81	$370.81	$322.24	$295.60	$279.69
$45,000	$534.16	$417.16	$362.52	$332.55	$314.65
$50,000	$593.51	$463.51	$402.80	$369.50	$349.61
$55,000	$652.86	$509.86	$443.08	$406.45	$384.57
$60,000	$712.22	$556.21	$483.36	$443.40	$419.53
$65,000	$771.57	$602.56	$523.64	$480.35	$454.49
$70,000	$830.92	$648.91	$563.92	$517.30	$489.46
$75,000	$890.27	$695.26	$604.20	$554.25	$524.42
$80,000	$949.62	$741.61	$644.48	$591.20	$559.38
$85,000	$1,008.97	$787.97	$684.76	$628.15	$594.34
$90,000	$1,068.32	$834.32	$725.04	$665.10	$629.30
$95,000	$1,127.67	$880.67	$765.32	$702.05	$664.26
$100,000	$1,187.02	$927.02	$805.60	$739.00	$699.22
$110,000	$1,305.72	$1,019.72	$886.16	$812.90	$769.14
$120,000	$1,424.43	$1,112.42	$966.72	$886.79	$839.06
$125,000	$1,483.78	$1,158.77	$1,007.00	$923.74	$874.02
$130,000	$1,543.13	$1,205.12	$1,047.28	$960.69	$908.98
$140,000	$1,661.83	$1,297.82	$1,127.84	$1,034.59	$978.91
$150,000	$1,780.53	$1,390.52	$1,208.39	$1,108.49	$1,048.83
$160,000	$1,899.23	$1,483.22	$1,288.95	$1,182.39	$1,118.75
$170,000	$2,017.94	$1,575.93	$1,369.51	$1,256.29	$1,188.67
$175,000	$2,077.29	$1,622.28	$1,409.79	$1,293.24	$1,223.63
$180,000	$2,136.64	$1,668.63	$1,450.07	$1,330.19	$1,258.59
$190,000	$2,255.34	$1,761.33	$1,530.63	$1,404.09	$1,328.51
$200,000	$2,374.04	$1,854.03	$1,611.19	$1,477.99	$1,398.43
$210,000	$2,492.74	$1,946.73	$1,691.75	$1,551.89	$1,468.36
$220,000	$2,611.44	$2,039.43	$1,772.31	$1,625.79	$1,538.28
$225,000	$2,670.79	$2,085.78	$1,812.59	$1,662.74	$1,573.24
$230,000	$2,730.15	$2,132.13	$1,852.87	$1,699.68	$1,608.20
$240,000	$2,848.85	$2,224.83	$1,933.43	$1,773.58	$1,678.12
$250,000	$2,967.55	$2,317.54	$2,013.99	$1,847.48	$1,748.04
$260,000	$3,086.25	$2,410.24	$2,094.55	$1,921.38	$1,817.96
$270,000	$3,204.95	$2,502.94	$2,175.11	$1,995.28	$1,887.88
$275,000	$3,264.30	$2,549.29	$2,215.39	$2,032.23	$1,922.84
$280,000	$3,323.65	$2,595.64	$2,255.67	$2,069.18	$1,957.81
$290,000	$3,442.36	$2,688.34	$2,336.23	$2,143.08	$2,027.73
$300,000	$3,561.06	$2,781.04	$2,416.78	$2,216.98	$2,097.65
$310,000	$3,679.76	$2,873.74	$2,497.34	$2,290.88	$2,167.57
$320,000	$3,798.46	$2,966.44	$2,577.90	$2,364.78	$2,237.49
$325,000	$3,857.81	$3,012.80	$2,618.18	$2,401.73	$2,272.45
$330,000	$3,917.16	$3,059.15	$2,658.46	$2,438.68	$2,307.41
$340,000	$4,035.87	$3,151.85	$2,739.02	$2,512.58	$2,377.33
$350,000	$4,154.57	$3,244.55	$2,819.58	$2,586.47	$2,447.26
$360,000	$4,273.27	$3,337.25	$2,900.14	$2,660.37	$2,517.18
$370,000	$4,391.97	$3,429.95	$2,980.70	$2,734.27	$2,587.10
$375,000	$4,451.32	$3,476.30	$3,020.98	$2,771.22	$2,622.06
$380,000	$4,510.67	$3,522.65	$3,061.26	$2,808.17	$2,657.02
$390,000	$4,629.37	$3,615.35	$3,141.82	$2,882.07	$2,726.94
$400,000	$4,748.08	$3,708.05	$3,222.38	$2,955.97	$2,796.86

With an interest rate of 7.75%, your monthly payment will be:

Loan Amount	Number of Years in Term				
	10	15	20	25	30
$1,000	$12.01	$9.42	$8.21	$7.56	$7.17
$2,000	$24.01	$18.83	$16.42	$15.11	$14.33
$3,000	$36.01	$28.24	$24.63	$22.66	$21.50
$4,000	$48.01	$37.66	$32.84	$30.22	$28.66
$5,000	$60.01	$47.07	$41.05	$37.77	$35.83
$6,000	$72.01	$56.48	$49.26	$45.32	$42.99
$7,000	$84.01	$65.89	$57.47	$52.88	$50.15
$8,000	$96.01	$75.31	$65.68	$60.43	$57.32
$9,000	$108.01	$84.72	$73.89	$67.98	$64.48
$10,000	$120.02	$94.13	$82.10	$75.54	$71.65
$15,000	$180.02	$141.20	$123.15	$113.30	$107.47
$20,000	$240.03	$188.26	$164.19	$151.07	$143.29
$25,000	$300.03	$235.32	$205.24	$188.84	$179.11
$30,000	$360.04	$282.39	$246.29	$226.60	$214.93
$35,000	$420.04	$329.45	$287.34	$264.37	$250.75
$40,000	$480.05	$376.52	$328.38	$302.14	$286.57
$45,000	$540.05	$423.58	$369.43	$339.90	$322.39
$50,000	$600.06	$470.64	$410.48	$377.67	$358.21
$55,000	$660.06	$517.71	$451.53	$415.44	$394.03
$60,000	$720.07	$564.77	$492.57	$453.20	$429.85
$65,000	$780.07	$611.83	$533.62	$490.97	$465.67
$70,000	$840.08	$658.90	$574.67	$528.74	$501.49
$75,000	$900.08	$705.96	$615.72	$566.50	$537.31
$80,000	$960.09	$753.03	$656.76	$604.27	$573.13
$85,000	$1,020.10	$800.09	$697.81	$642.03	$608.96
$90,000	$1,080.10	$847.15	$738.86	$679.80	$644.78
$95,000	$1,140.11	$894.22	$779.91	$717.57	$680.60
$100,000	$1,200.11	$941.28	$820.95	$755.33	$716.42
$110,000	$1,320.12	$1,035.41	$903.05	$830.87	$788.06
$120,000	$1,440.13	$1,129.54	$985.14	$906.40	$859.70
$125,000	$1,500.14	$1,176.60	$1,026.19	$944.17	$895.52
$130,000	$1,560.14	$1,223.66	$1,067.24	$981.93	$931.34
$140,000	$1,680.15	$1,317.79	$1,149.33	$1,057.47	$1,002.98
$150,000	$1,800.16	$1,411.92	$1,231.43	$1,133.00	$1,074.62
$160,000	$1,920.18	$1,506.05	$1,313.52	$1,208.53	$1,146.26
$170,000	$2,040.19	$1,600.17	$1,395.62	$1,284.06	$1,217.91
$175,000	$2,100.19	$1,647.24	$1,436.66	$1,321.83	$1,253.73
$180,000	$2,160.20	$1,694.30	$1,477.71	$1,359.60	$1,289.55
$190,000	$2,280.21	$1,788.43	$1,559.81	$1,435.13	$1,361.19
$200,000	$2,400.22	$1,882.56	$1,641.90	$1,510.66	$1,432.83
$210,000	$2,520.23	$1,976.68	$1,724.00	$1,586.20	$1,504.47
$220,000	$2,640.24	$2,070.81	$1,806.09	$1,661.73	$1,576.11
$225,000	$2,700.24	$2,117.88	$1,847.14	$1,699.49	$1,611.93
$230,000	$2,760.25	$2,164.94	$1,888.19	$1,737.26	$1,647.75
$240,000	$2,880.26	$2,259.07	$1,970.28	$1,812.79	$1,719.39
$250,000	$3,000.27	$2,353.19	$2,052.38	$1,888.33	$1,791.04
$260,000	$3,120.28	$2,447.32	$2,134.47	$1,963.86	$1,862.68
$270,000	$3,240.29	$2,541.45	$2,216.57	$2,039.39	$1,934.32
$275,000	$3,300.30	$2,588.51	$2,257.61	$2,077.16	$1,970.14
$280,000	$3,360.30	$2,635.58	$2,298.66	$2,114.93	$2,005.96
$290,000	$3,480.31	$2,729.70	$2,380.76	$2,190.46	$2,077.60
$300,000	$3,600.32	$2,823.83	$2,462.85	$2,265.99	$2,149.24

With an interest rate of 7.75%, your monthly payment will be:

Loan Amount	Number of Years in Term				
	10	15	20	25	30
$310,000	$3,720.33	$2,917.96	$2,544.95	$2,341.52	$2,220.88
$320,000	$3,840.35	$3,012.09	$2,627.04	$2,417.06	$2,292.52
$325,000	$3,900.35	$3,059.15	$2,668.09	$2,454.82	$2,328.34
$330,000	$3,960.36	$3,106.21	$2,709.14	$2,492.59	$2,364.17
$340,000	$4,080.37	$3,200.34	$2,791.23	$2,568.12	$2,435.81
$350,000	$4,200.38	$3,294.47	$2,873.32	$2,643.66	$2,507.45
$360,000	$4,320.39	$3,388.60	$2,955.42	$2,719.19	$2,579.09
$370,000	$4,440.40	$3,482.73	$3,037.51	$2,794.72	$2,650.73
$375,000	$4,500.40	$3,529.79	$3,078.56	$2,832.49	$2,686.55
$380,000	$4,560.41	$3,576.85	$3,119.61	$2,870.25	$2,722.37
$390,000	$4,680.42	$3,670.98	$3,201.70	$2,945.79	$2,794.01
$400,000	$4,800.43	$3,765.11	$3,283.80	$3,021.32	$2,865.65

With an interest rate of 8.00%, your monthly payment will be:

Loan Amount	Number of Years in Term				
	10	15	20	25	30
$1,000	$12.14	$9.56	$8.37	$7.72	$7.34
$2,000	$24.27	$19.12	$16.73	$15.44	$14.68
$3,000	$36.40	$28.67	$25.10	$23.16	$22.02
$4,000	$48.54	$38.23	$33.46	$30.88	$29.36
$5,000	$60.67	$47.79	$41.83	$38.60	$36.69
$6,000	$72.80	$57.34	$50.19	$46.31	$44.03
$7,000	$84.93	$66.90	$58.56	$54.03	$51.37
$8,000	$97.07	$76.46	$66.92	$61.75	$58.71
$9,000	$109.20	$86.01	$75.28	$69.47	$66.04
$10,000	$121.33	$95.57	$83.65	$77.19	$73.38
$15,000	$182.00	$143.35	$125.47	$115.78	$110.07
$20,000	$242.66	$191.14	$167.29	$154.37	$146.76
$25,000	$303.32	$238.92	$209.12	$192.96	$183.45
$30,000	$363.99	$286.70	$250.94	$231.55	$220.13
$35,000	$424.65	$334.48	$292.76	$270.14	$256.82
$40,000	$485.32	$382.27	$334.58	$308.73	$293.51
$45,000	$545.98	$430.05	$376.40	$347.32	$330.20
$50,000	$606.64	$477.83	$418.23	$385.91	$366.89
$55,000	$667.31	$525.61	$460.05	$424.50	$403.58
$60,000	$727.97	$573.40	$501.87	$463.09	$440.26
$65,000	$788.63	$621.18	$543.69	$501.69	$476.95
$70,000	$849.30	$668.96	$585.51	$540.28	$513.64
$75,000	$909.96	$716.74	$627.34	$578.87	$550.33
$80,000	$970.63	$764.53	$669.16	$617.46	$587.02
$85,000	$1,031.29	$812.31	$710.98	$656.05	$623.70
$90,000	$1,091.95	$860.09	$752.80	$694.64	$660.39
$95,000	$1,152.62	$907.87	$794.62	$733.23	$697.08
$100,000	$1,213.28	$955.66	$836.45	$771.82	$733.77
$110,000	$1,334.61	$1,051.22	$920.09	$849.00	$807.15
$120,000	$1,455.94	$1,146.79	$1,003.73	$926.18	$880.52
$125,000	$1,516.60	$1,194.57	$1,045.56	$964.78	$917.21
$130,000	$1,577.26	$1,242.35	$1,087.38	$1,003.37	$953.90
$140,000	$1,698.59	$1,337.92	$1,171.02	$1,080.55	$1,027.28
$150,000	$1,819.92	$1,433.48	$1,254.67	$1,157.73	$1,100.65

With an interest rate of 8.00%, your monthly payment will be:

Loan Amount	Number of Years in Term				
	10	15	20	25	30
$160,000	$1,941.25	$1,529.05	$1,338.31	$1,234.91	$1,174.03
$170,000	$2,062.57	$1,624.61	$1,421.95	$1,312.09	$1,247.40
$175,000	$2,123.24	$1,672.40	$1,463.78	$1,350.68	$1,284.09
$180,000	$2,183.90	$1,720.18	$1,505.60	$1,389.27	$1,320.78
$190,000	$2,305.23	$1,815.74	$1,589.24	$1,466.46	$1,394.16
$200,000	$2,426.56	$1,911.31	$1,672.89	$1,543.64	$1,467.53
$210,000	$2,547.88	$2,006.87	$1,756.53	$1,620.82	$1,540.91
$220,000	$2,669.21	$2,102.44	$1,840.17	$1,698.00	$1,614.29
$225,000	$2,729.88	$2,150.22	$1,882.00	$1,736.59	$1,650.98
$230,000	$2,790.54	$2,198.00	$1,923.82	$1,775.18	$1,687.66
$240,000	$2,911.87	$2,293.57	$2,007.46	$1,852.36	$1,761.04
$250,000	$3,033.19	$2,389.14	$2,091.11	$1,929.55	$1,834.42
$260,000	$3,154.52	$2,484.70	$2,174.75	$2,006.73	$1,907.79
$270,000	$3,275.85	$2,580.27	$2,258.39	$2,083.91	$1,981.17
$275,000	$3,336.51	$2,628.05	$2,300.22	$2,122.50	$2,017.86
$280,000	$3,397.18	$2,675.83	$2,342.04	$2,161.09	$2,054.55
$290,000	$3,518.51	$2,771.40	$2,425.68	$2,238.27	$2,127.92
$300,000	$3,639.83	$2,866.96	$2,509.33	$2,315.45	$2,201.30
$310,000	$3,761.16	$2,962.53	$2,592.97	$2,392.64	$2,274.68
$320,000	$3,882.49	$3,058.09	$2,676.61	$2,469.82	$2,348.05
$325,000	$3,943.15	$3,105.87	$2,718.44	$2,508.41	$2,384.74
$330,000	$4,003.82	$3,153.66	$2,760.26	$2,547.00	$2,421.43
$340,000	$4,125.14	$3,249.22	$2,843.90	$2,624.18	$2,494.80
$350,000	$4,246.47	$3,344.79	$2,927.55	$2,701.36	$2,568.18
$360,000	$4,367.80	$3,440.35	$3,011.19	$2,778.54	$2,641.56
$370,000	$4,489.13	$3,535.92	$3,094.83	$2,855.73	$2,714.93
$375,000	$4,549.79	$3,583.70	$3,136.66	$2,894.32	$2,751.62
$380,000	$4,610.45	$3,631.48	$3,178.48	$2,932.91	$2,788.31
$390,000	$4,731.78	$3,727.05	$3,262.12	$3,010.09	$2,861.69
$400,000	$4,853.11	$3,822.61	$3,345.77	$3,087.27	$2,935.06

With an interest rate of 8.25%, your monthly payment will be:

Loan Amount	Number of Years in Term				
	10	15	20	25	30
$1,000	$12.27	$9.71	$8.53	$7.89	$7.52
$2,000	$24.54	$19.41	$17.05	$15.77	$15.03
$3,000	$36.80	$29.11	$25.57	$23.66	$22.54
$4,000	$49.07	$38.81	$34.09	$31.54	$30.06
$5,000	$61.33	$48.51	$42.61	$39.43	$37.57
$6,000	$73.60	$58.21	$51.13	$47.31	$45.08
$7,000	$85.86	$67.91	$59.65	$55.20	$52.59
$8,000	$98.13	$77.62	$68.17	$63.08	$60.11
$9,000	$110.39	$87.32	$76.69	$70.97	$67.62
$10,000	$122.66	$97.02	$85.21	$78.85	$75.13
$15,000	$183.98	$145.53	$127.81	$118.27	$112.69
$20,000	$245.31	$194.03	$170.42	$157.70	$150.26
$25,000	$306.64	$242.54	$213.02	$197.12	$187.82
$30,000	$367.96	$291.05	$255.62	$236.54	$225.38

With an interest rate of 8.25%, your monthly payment will be:

Loan Amount	Number of Years in Term				
	10	15	20	25	30
$35,000	$429.29	$339.55	$298.23	$275.96	$262.95
$40,000	$490.62	$388.06	$340.83	$315.39	$300.51
$45,000	$551.94	$436.57	$383.43	$354.81	$338.07
$50,000	$613.27	$485.08	$426.04	$394.23	$375.64
$55,000	$674.59	$533.58	$468.64	$433.65	$413.20
$60,000	$735.92	$582.09	$511.24	$473.08	$450.76
$65,000	$797.25	$630.60	$553.85	$512.50	$488.33
$70,000	$858.57	$679.10	$596.45	$551.92	$525.89
$75,000	$919.90	$727.61	$639.05	$591.34	$563.45
$80,000	$981.23	$776.12	$681.66	$630.77	$601.02
$85,000	$1,042.55	$824.62	$724.26	$670.19	$638.58
$90,000	$1,103.88	$873.13	$766.86	$709.61	$676.14
$95,000	$1,165.20	$921.64	$809.47	$749.03	$713.71
$100,000	$1,226.53	$970.15	$852.07	$788.46	$751.27
$110,000	$1,349.18	$1,067.16	$937.28	$867.30	$826.40
$120,000	$1,471.84	$1,164.17	$1,022.48	$946.15	$901.52
$125,000	$1,533.16	$1,212.68	$1,065.09	$985.57	$939.09
$130,000	$1,594.49	$1,261.19	$1,107.69	$1,024.99	$976.65
$140,000	$1,717.14	$1,358.20	$1,192.90	$1,103.84	$1,051.78
$150,000	$1,839.79	$1,455.22	$1,278.10	$1,182.68	$1,126.90
$160,000	$1,962.45	$1,552.23	$1,363.31	$1,261.53	$1,202.03
$170,000	$2,085.10	$1,649.24	$1,448.52	$1,340.37	$1,277.16
$175,000	$2,146.43	$1,697.75	$1,491.12	$1,379.79	$1,314.72
$180,000	$2,207.75	$1,746.26	$1,533.72	$1,419.22	$1,352.28
$190,000	$2,330.40	$1,843.27	$1,618.93	$1,498.06	$1,427.41
$200,000	$2,453.06	$1,940.29	$1,704.14	$1,576.91	$1,502.54
$210,000	$2,575.71	$2,037.30	$1,789.34	$1,655.75	$1,577.66
$220,000	$2,698.36	$2,134.31	$1,874.55	$1,734.60	$1,652.79
$225,000	$2,759.69	$2,182.82	$1,917.15	$1,774.02	$1,690.35
$230,000	$2,821.02	$2,231.33	$1,959.76	$1,813.44	$1,727.92
$240,000	$2,943.67	$2,328.34	$2,044.96	$1,892.29	$1,803.04
$250,000	$3,066.32	$2,425.36	$2,130.17	$1,971.13	$1,878.17
$260,000	$3,188.97	$2,522.37	$2,215.38	$2,049.98	$1,953.30
$270,000	$3,311.63	$2,619.38	$2,300.58	$2,128.82	$2,028.42
$275,000	$3,372.95	$2,667.89	$2,343.19	$2,168.24	$2,065.99
$280,000	$3,434.28	$2,716.40	$2,385.79	$2,207.67	$2,103.55
$290,000	$3,556.93	$2,813.41	$2,471.00	$2,286.51	$2,178.68
$300,000	$3,679.58	$2,910.43	$2,556.20	$2,365.36	$2,253.80
$310,000	$3,802.24	$3,007.44	$2,641.41	$2,444.20	$2,328.93
$320,000	$3,924.89	$3,104.45	$2,726.62	$2,523.05	$2,404.06
$325,000	$3,986.22	$3,152.96	$2,769.22	$2,562.47	$2,441.62
$330,000	$4,047.54	$3,201.47	$2,811.82	$2,601.89	$2,479.18
$340,000	$4,170.19	$3,298.48	$2,897.03	$2,680.74	$2,554.31
$350,000	$4,292.85	$3,395.50	$2,982.23	$2,759.58	$2,629.44
$360,000	$4,415.50	$3,492.51	$3,067.44	$2,838.43	$2,704.56
$370,000	$4,538.15	$3,589.52	$3,152.65	$2,917.27	$2,779.69
$375,000	$4,599.48	$3,638.03	$3,195.25	$2,956.69	$2,817.25
$380,000	$4,660.80	$3,686.54	$3,237.85	$2,996.12	$2,854.82
$390,000	$4,783.46	$3,783.55	$3,323.06	$3,074.96	$2,929.94
$400,000	$4,906.11	$3,880.57	$3,408.27	$3,153.81	$3,005.07

With an interest rate of 8.5%, your monthly payment will be:

Loan Amount	Number of Years in Term				
	10	15	20	25	30
$1,000	$12.40	$9.85	$8.68	$8.06	$7.69
$2,000	$24.80	$19.70	$17.36	$16.11	$15.38
$3,000	$37.20	$29.55	$26.04	$24.16	$23.07
$4,000	$49.60	$39.39	$34.72	$32.21	$30.76
$5,000	$62.00	$49.24	$43.40	$40.27	$38.45
$6,000	$74.40	$59.09	$52.07	$48.32	$46.14
$7,000	$86.79	$68.94	$60.75	$56.37	$53.83
$8,000	$99.19	$78.78	$69.43	$64.42	$61.52
$9,000	$111.59	$88.63	$78.11	$72.48	$69.21
$10,000	$123.99	$98.48	$86.79	$80.53	$76.90
$15,000	$185.98	$147.72	$130.18	$120.79	$115.34
$20,000	$247.98	$196.95	$173.57	$161.05	$153.79
$25,000	$309.97	$246.19	$216.96	$201.31	$192.23
$30,000	$371.96	$295.43	$260.35	$241.57	$230.68
$35,000	$433.95	$344.66	$303.74	$281.83	$269.12
$40,000	$495.95	$393.90	$347.13	$322.10	$307.57
$45,000	$557.94	$443.14	$390.53	$362.36	$346.02
$50,000	$619.93	$492.37	$433.92	$402.62	$384.46
$55,000	$681.93	$541.61	$477.31	$442.88	$422.91
$60,000	$743.92	$590.85	$520.70	$483.14	$461.35
$65,000	$805.91	$640.09	$564.09	$523.40	$499.80
$70,000	$867.90	$689.32	$607.48	$563.66	$538.24
$75,000	$929.90	$738.56	$650.87	$603.93	$576.69
$80,000	$991.89	$787.80	$694.26	$644.19	$615.14
$85,000	$1,053.88	$837.03	$737.65	$684.45	$653.58
$90,000	$1,115.88	$886.27	$781.05	$724.71	$692.03
$95,000	$1,177.87	$935.51	$824.44	$764.97	$730.47
$100,000	$1,239.86	$984.74	$867.83	$805.23	$768.92
$110,000	$1,363.85	$1,083.22	$954.61	$885.75	$845.81
$120,000	$1,487.83	$1,181.69	$1,041.39	$966.28	$922.70
$125,000	$1,549.83	$1,230.93	$1,084.78	$1,006.54	$961.15
$130,000	$1,611.82	$1,280.17	$1,128.18	$1,046.80	$999.59
$140,000	$1,735.80	$1,378.64	$1,214.96	$1,127.32	$1,076.48
$150,000	$1,859.79	$1,477.11	$1,301.74	$1,207.85	$1,153.38
$160,000	$1,983.78	$1,575.59	$1,388.52	$1,288.37	$1,230.27
$170,000	$2,107.76	$1,674.06	$1,475.30	$1,368.89	$1,307.16
$175,000	$2,169.75	$1,723.30	$1,518.70	$1,409.15	$1,345.60
$180,000	$2,231.75	$1,772.54	$1,562.09	$1,449.41	$1,384.05
$190,000	$2,355.73	$1,871.01	$1,648.87	$1,529.94	$1,460.94
$200,000	$2,479.72	$1,969.48	$1,735.65	$1,610.46	$1,537.83
$210,000	$2,603.70	$2,067.96	$1,822.43	$1,690.98	$1,614.72
$220,000	$2,727.69	$2,166.43	$1,909.22	$1,771.50	$1,691.61
$225,000	$2,789.68	$2,215.67	$1,952.61	$1,811.77	$1,730.06
$230,000	$2,851.68	$2,264.91	$1,996.00	$1,852.03	$1,768.51
$240,000	$2,975.66	$2,363.38	$2,082.78	$1,932.55	$1,845.40
$250,000	$3,099.65	$2,461.85	$2,169.56	$2,013.07	$1,922.29
$260,000	$3,223.63	$2,560.33	$2,256.35	$2,093.60	$1,999.18
$270,000	$3,347.62	$2,658.80	$2,343.13	$2,174.12	$2,076.07
$275,000	$3,409.61	$2,708.04	$2,386.52	$2,214.38	$2,114.52
$280,000	$3,471.60	$2,757.28	$2,429.91	$2,254.64	$2,152.96
$290,000	$3,595.59	$2,855.75	$2,516.69	$2,335.16	$2,229.85
$300,000	$3,719.58	$2,954.22	$2,603.47	$2,415.69	$2,306.75

With an interest rate of 8.5%, your monthly payment will be:

Loan Amount	Number of Years in Term				
	10	15	20	25	30
$310,000	$3,843.56	$3,052.70	$2,690.26	$2,496.21	$2,383.64
$320,000	$3,967.55	$3,151.17	$2,777.04	$2,576.73	$2,460.53
$325,000	$4,029.54	$3,200.41	$2,820.43	$2,616.99	$2,498.97
$330,000	$4,091.53	$3,249.65	$2,863.82	$2,657.25	$2,537.42
$340,000	$4,215.52	$3,348.12	$2,950.60	$2,737.78	$2,614.31
$350,000	$4,339.50	$3,446.59	$3,037.39	$2,818.30	$2,691.20
$360,000	$4,463.49	$3,545.07	$3,124.17	$2,898.82	$2,768.09
$370,000	$4,587.48	$3,643.54	$3,210.95	$2,979.35	$2,844.98
$375,000	$4,649.47	$3,692.78	$3,254.34	$3,019.61	$2,883.43
$380,000	$4,711.46	$3,742.02	$3,297.73	$3,059.87	$2,921.88
$390,000	$4,835.45	$3,840.49	$3,384.52	$3,140.39	$2,998.77
$400,000	$4,959.43	$3,938.96	$3,471.30	$3,220.91	$3,075.66

With an interest rate of 8.75%, your monthly payment will be:

Loan Amount	Number of Years in Term				
	10	15	20	25	30
$1,000	$12.54	$10.00	$8.84	$8.23	$7.87
$2,000	$25.07	$19.99	$17.68	$16.45	$15.74
$3,000	$37.60	$29.99	$26.52	$24.67	$23.61
$4,000	$50.14	$39.98	$35.35	$32.89	$31.47
$5,000	$62.67	$49.98	$44.19	$41.11	$39.34
$6,000	$75.20	$59.97	$53.03	$49.33	$47.21
$7,000	$87.73	$69.97	$61.86	$57.56	$55.07
$8,000	$100.27	$79.96	$70.70	$65.78	$62.94
$9,000	$112.80	$89.96	$79.54	$74.00	$70.81
$10,000	$125.33	$99.95	$88.38	$82.22	$78.68
$15,000	$188.00	$149.92	$132.56	$123.33	$118.01
$20,000	$250.66	$199.89	$176.75	$164.43	$157.35
$25,000	$313.32	$249.87	$220.93	$205.54	$196.68
$30,000	$375.99	$299.84	$265.12	$246.65	$236.02
$35,000	$438.65	$349.81	$309.30	$287.76	$275.35
$40,000	$501.31	$399.78	$353.49	$328.86	$314.69
$45,000	$563.98	$449.76	$397.67	$369.97	$354.02
$50,000	$626.64	$499.73	$441.86	$411.08	$393.36
$55,000	$689.30	$549.70	$486.05	$452.18	$432.69
$60,000	$751.97	$599.67	$530.23	$493.29	$472.03
$65,000	$814.63	$649.65	$574.42	$534.40	$511.36
$70,000	$877.29	$699.62	$618.60	$575.51	$550.70
$75,000	$939.96	$749.59	$662.79	$616.61	$590.03
$80,000	$1,002.62	$799.56	$706.97	$657.72	$629.37
$85,000	$1,065.28	$849.54	$751.16	$698.83	$668.70
$90,000	$1,127.95	$899.51	$795.34	$739.93	$708.04
$95,000	$1,190.61	$949.48	$839.53	$781.04	$747.37
$100,000	$1,253.27	$999.45	$883.72	$822.15	$786.71
$110,000	$1,378.60	$1,099.40	$972.09	$904.36	$865.38
$120,000	$1,503.93	$1,199.34	$1,060.46	$986.58	$944.05
$125,000	$1,566.59	$1,249.32	$1,104.64	$1,027.68	$983.38
$130,000	$1,629.25	$1,299.29	$1,148.83	$1,068.79	$1,022.72
$140,000	$1,754.58	$1,399.23	$1,237.20	$1,151.01	$1,101.39
$150,000	$1,879.91	$1,499.18	$1,325.57	$1,233.22	$1,180.06

With an interest rate of 8.75%, your monthly payment will be:

Loan Amount	Number of Years in Term				
	10	15	20	25	30
$160,000	$2,005.23	$1,599.12	$1,413.94	$1,315.43	$1,258.73
$170,000	$2,130.56	$1,699.07	$1,502.31	$1,397.65	$1,337.40
$175,000	$2,193.22	$1,749.04	$1,546.50	$1,438.76	$1,376.73
$180,000	$2,255.89	$1,799.01	$1,590.68	$1,479.86	$1,416.07
$190,000	$2,381.21	$1,898.96	$1,679.06	$1,562.08	$1,494.74
$200,000	$2,506.54	$1,998.90	$1,767.43	$1,644.29	$1,573.41
$210,000	$2,631.87	$2,098.85	$1,855.80	$1,726.51	$1,652.08
$220,000	$2,757.19	$2,198.79	$1,944.17	$1,808.72	$1,730.75
$225,000	$2,819.86	$2,248.76	$1,988.35	$1,849.83	$1,770.08
$230,000	$2,882.52	$2,298.74	$2,032.54	$1,890.94	$1,809.42
$240,000	$3,007.85	$2,398.68	$2,120.91	$1,973.15	$1,888.09
$250,000	$3,133.17	$2,498.63	$2,209.28	$2,055.36	$1,966.76
$260,000	$3,258.50	$2,598.57	$2,297.65	$2,137.58	$2,045.43
$270,000	$3,383.83	$2,698.52	$2,386.02	$2,219.79	$2,124.10
$275,000	$3,446.49	$2,748.49	$2,430.21	$2,260.90	$2,163.43
$280,000	$3,509.15	$2,798.46	$2,474.39	$2,302.01	$2,202.77
$290,000	$3,634.48	$2,898.41	$2,562.77	$2,384.22	$2,281.44
$300,000	$3,759.81	$2,998.35	$2,651.14	$2,466.44	$2,360.11
$310,000	$3,885.13	$3,098.30	$2,739.51	$2,548.65	$2,438.78
$320,000	$4,010.46	$3,198.24	$2,827.88	$2,630.86	$2,517.45
$325,000	$4,073.12	$3,248.21	$2,872.06	$2,671.97	$2,556.78
$330,000	$4,135.79	$3,298.19	$2,916.25	$2,713.08	$2,596.12
$340,000	$4,261.11	$3,398.13	$3,004.62	$2,795.29	$2,674.79
$350,000	$4,386.44	$3,498.08	$3,092.99	$2,877.51	$2,753.46
$360,000	$4,511.77	$3,598.02	$3,181.36	$2,959.72	$2,832.13
$370,000	$4,637.09	$3,697.97	$3,269.73	$3,041.94	$2,910.80
$375,000	$4,699.76	$3,747.94	$3,313.92	$3,083.04	$2,950.13
$380,000	$4,762.42	$3,797.91	$3,358.11	$3,124.15	$2,989.47
$390,000	$4,887.75	$3,897.85	$3,446.48	$3,206.37	$3,068.14
$400,000	$5,013.08	$3,997.80	$3,534.85	$3,288.58	$3,146.81

With an interest rate of 9.00%, your monthly payment will be:

Loan Amount	Number of Years in Term				
	10	15	20	25	30
$1,000	$12.67	$10.15	$9.00	$8.40	$8.05
$2,000	$25.34	$20.29	$18.00	$16.79	$16.10
$3,000	$38.01	$30.43	$27.00	$25.18	$24.14
$4,000	$50.68	$40.58	$35.99	$33.57	$32.19
$5,000	$63.34	$50.72	$44.99	$41.96	$40.24
$6,000	$76.01	$60.86	$53.99	$50.36	$48.28
$7,000	$88.68	$71.00	$62.99	$58.75	$56.33
$8,000	$101.35	$81.15	$71.98	$67.14	$64.37
$9,000	$114.01	$91.29	$80.98	$75.53	$72.42
$10,000	$126.68	$101.43	$89.98	$83.92	$80.47
$15,000	$190.02	$152.14	$134.96	$125.88	$120.70
$20,000	$253.36	$202.86	$179.95	$167.84	$160.93
$25,000	$316.69	$253.57	$224.94	$209.80	$201.16
$30,000	$380.03	$304.28	$269.92	$251.76	$241.39

With an interest rate of 9.00%, your monthly payment will be:

Loan Amount	Number of Years in Term				
	10	15	20	25	30
$35,000	$443.37	$355.00	$314.91	$293.72	$281.62
$40,000	$506.71	$405.71	$359.90	$335.68	$321.85
$45,000	$570.05	$456.42	$404.88	$377.64	$362.09
$50,000	$633.38	$507.14	$449.87	$419.60	$402.32
$55,000	$696.72	$557.85	$494.85	$461.56	$442.55
$60,000	$760.06	$608.56	$539.84	$503.52	$482.78
$65,000	$823.40	$659.28	$584.83	$545.48	$523.01
$70,000	$886.74	$709.99	$629.81	$587.44	$563.24
$75,000	$950.07	$760.70	$674.80	$629.40	$603.47
$80,000	$1,013.41	$811.42	$719.79	$671.36	$643.70
$85,000	$1,076.75	$862.13	$764.77	$713.32	$683.93
$90,000	$1,140.09	$912.84	$809.76	$755.28	$724.17
$95,000	$1,203.42	$963.56	$854.74	$797.24	$764.40
$100,000	$1,266.76	$1,014.27	$899.73	$839.20	$804.63
$110,000	$1,393.44	$1,115.70	$989.70	$923.12	$885.09
$120,000	$1,520.11	$1,217.12	$1,079.68	$1,007.04	$965.55
$125,000	$1,583.45	$1,267.84	$1,124.66	$1,049.00	$1,005.78
$130,000	$1,646.79	$1,318.55	$1,169.65	$1,090.96	$1,046.01
$140,000	$1,773.47	$1,419.98	$1,259.62	$1,174.88	$1,126.48
$150,000	$1,900.14	$1,521.40	$1,349.59	$1,258.80	$1,206.94
$160,000	$2,026.82	$1,622.83	$1,439.57	$1,342.72	$1,287.40
$170,000	$2,153.49	$1,724.26	$1,529.54	$1,426.64	$1,367.86
$175,000	$2,216.83	$1,774.97	$1,574.53	$1,468.60	$1,408.09
$180,000	$2,280.17	$1,825.68	$1,619.51	$1,510.56	$1,448.33
$190,000	$2,406.84	$1,927.11	$1,709.48	$1,594.48	$1,528.79
$200,000	$2,533.52	$2,028.54	$1,799.46	$1,678.40	$1,609.25
$210,000	$2,660.20	$2,129.96	$1,889.43	$1,762.32	$1,689.71
$220,000	$2,786.87	$2,231.39	$1,979.40	$1,846.24	$1,770.17
$225,000	$2,850.21	$2,282.10	$2,024.39	$1,888.20	$1,810.41
$230,000	$2,913.55	$2,332.82	$2,069.37	$1,930.16	$1,850.64
$240,000	$3,040.22	$2,434.24	$2,159.35	$2,014.08	$1,931.10
$250,000	$3,166.90	$2,535.67	$2,249.32	$2,098.00	$2,011.56
$260,000	$3,293.58	$2,637.10	$2,339.29	$2,181.92	$2,092.02
$270,000	$3,420.25	$2,738.52	$2,429.27	$2,265.84	$2,172.49
$275,000	$3,483.59	$2,789.24	$2,474.25	$2,307.79	$2,212.72
$280,000	$3,546.93	$2,839.95	$2,519.24	$2,349.75	$2,252.95
$290,000	$3,673.60	$2,941.38	$2,609.21	$2,433.67	$2,333.41
$300,000	$3,800.28	$3,042.80	$2,699.18	$2,517.59	$2,413.87
$310,000	$3,926.95	$3,144.23	$2,789.16	$2,601.51	$2,494.34
$320,000	$4,053.63	$3,245.66	$2,879.13	$2,685.43	$2,574.80
$325,000	$4,116.97	$3,296.37	$2,924.11	$2,727.39	$2,615.03
$330,000	$4,180.31	$3,347.08	$2,969.10	$2,769.35	$2,655.26
$340,000	$4,306.98	$3,448.51	$3,059.07	$2,853.27	$2,735.72
$350,000	$4,433.66	$3,549.94	$3,149.05	$2,937.19	$2,816.18
$360,000	$4,560.33	$3,651.36	$3,239.02	$3,021.11	$2,896.65
$370,000	$4,687.01	$3,752.79	$3,328.99	$3,105.03	$2,977.11
$375,000	$4,750.35	$3,803.50	$3,373.98	$3,146.99	$3,017.34
$380,000	$4,813.68	$3,854.22	$3,418.96	$3,188.95	$3,057.57
$390,000	$4,940.36	$3,955.64	$3,508.94	$3,272.87	$3,138.03
$400,000	$5,067.04	$4,057.07	$3,598.91	$3,356.79	$3,218.50

With an interest rate of 9.25%, your monthly payment will be:

Loan Amount	Number of Years in Term				
	10	15	20	25	30
$1,000	$12.81	$10.30	$9.16	$8.57	$8.23
$2,000	$25.61	$20.59	$18.32	$17.13	$16.46
$3,000	$38.41	$30.88	$27.48	$25.70	$24.69
$4,000	$51.22	$41.17	$36.64	$34.26	$32.91
$5,000	$64.02	$51.46	$45.80	$42.82	$41.14
$6,000	$76.82	$61.76	$54.96	$51.39	$49.37
$7,000	$89.63	$72.05	$64.12	$59.95	$57.59
$8,000	$102.43	$82.34	$73.27	$68.52	$65.82
$9,000	$115.23	$92.63	$82.43	$77.08	$74.05
$10,000	$128.04	$102.92	$91.59	$85.64	$82.27
$15,000	$192.05	$154.38	$137.39	$128.46	$123.41
$20,000	$256.07	$205.84	$183.18	$171.28	$164.54
$25,000	$320.09	$257.30	$228.97	$214.10	$205.67
$30,000	$384.10	$308.76	$274.77	$256.92	$246.81
$35,000	$448.12	$360.22	$320.56	$299.74	$287.94
$40,000	$512.14	$411.68	$366.35	$342.56	$329.08
$45,000	$576.15	$463.14	$412.15	$385.38	$370.21
$50,000	$640.17	$514.60	$457.94	$428.20	$411.34
$55,000	$704.18	$566.06	$503.73	$471.02	$452.48
$60,000	$768.20	$617.52	$549.53	$513.83	$493.61
$65,000	$832.22	$668.98	$595.32	$556.65	$534.74
$70,000	$896.23	$720.44	$641.11	$599.47	$575.88
$75,000	$960.25	$771.90	$686.91	$642.29	$617.01
$80,000	$1,024.27	$823.36	$732.70	$685.11	$658.15
$85,000	$1,088.28	$874.82	$778.49	$727.93	$699.28
$90,000	$1,152.30	$926.28	$824.29	$770.75	$740.41
$95,000	$1,216.32	$977.74	$870.08	$813.57	$781.55
$100,000	$1,280.33	$1,029.20	$915.87	$856.39	$822.68
$110,000	$1,408.36	$1,132.12	$1,007.46	$942.03	$904.95
$120,000	$1,536.40	$1,235.04	$1,099.05	$1,027.66	$987.22
$125,000	$1,600.41	$1,286.50	$1,144.84	$1,070.48	$1,028.35
$130,000	$1,664.43	$1,337.95	$1,190.63	$1,113.30	$1,069.48
$140,000	$1,792.46	$1,440.87	$1,282.22	$1,198.94	$1,151.75
$150,000	$1,920.50	$1,543.79	$1,373.81	$1,284.58	$1,234.02
$160,000	$2,048.53	$1,646.71	$1,465.39	$1,370.22	$1,316.29
$170,000	$2,176.56	$1,749.63	$1,556.98	$1,455.85	$1,398.55
$175,000	$2,240.58	$1,801.09	$1,602.77	$1,498.67	$1,439.69
$180,000	$2,304.59	$1,852.55	$1,648.57	$1,541.49	$1,480.82
$190,000	$2,432.63	$1,955.47	$1,740.15	$1,627.13	$1,563.09
$200,000	$2,560.66	$2,058.39	$1,831.74	$1,712.77	$1,645.36
$210,000	$2,688.69	$2,161.31	$1,923.33	$1,798.41	$1,727.62
$220,000	$2,816.72	$2,264.23	$2,014.91	$1,884.05	$1,809.89
$225,000	$2,880.74	$2,315.69	$2,060.71	$1,926.86	$1,851.02
$230,000	$2,944.76	$2,367.15	$2,106.50	$1,969.68	$1,892.16
$240,000	$3,072.79	$2,470.07	$2,198.09	$2,055.32	$1,974.43
$250,000	$3,200.82	$2,572.99	$2,289.67	$2,140.96	$2,056.69
$260,000	$3,328.86	$2,675.90	$2,381.26	$2,226.60	$2,138.96
$270,000	$3,456.89	$2,778.82	$2,472.85	$2,312.24	$2,221.23
$275,000	$3,520.90	$2,830.28	$2,518.64	$2,355.06	$2,262.36
$280,000	$3,584.92	$2,881.74	$2,564.43	$2,397.87	$2,303.50
$290,000	$3,712.95	$2,984.66	$2,656.02	$2,483.51	$2,385.76
$300,000	$3,840.99	$3,087.58	$2,747.61	$2,569.15	$2,468.03

With an interest rate of 9.25%, your monthly payment will be:

Loan Amount	Number of Years in Term				
	10	15	20	25	30
$310,000	$3,969.02	$3,190.50	$2,839.19	$2,654.79	$2,550.30
$320,000	$4,097.05	$3,293.42	$2,930.78	$2,740.43	$2,632.57
$325,000	$4,161.07	$3,344.88	$2,976.57	$2,783.25	$2,673.70
$330,000	$4,225.08	$3,396.34	$3,022.37	$2,826.07	$2,714.83
$340,000	$4,353.12	$3,499.26	$3,113.95	$2,911.70	$2,797.10
$350,000	$4,481.15	$3,602.18	$3,205.54	$2,997.34	$2,879.37
$360,000	$4,609.18	$3,705.10	$3,297.13	$3,082.98	$2,961.64
$370,000	$4,737.22	$3,808.02	$3,388.71	$3,168.62	$3,043.90
$375,000	$4,801.23	$3,859.48	$3,434.51	$3,211.44	$3,085.04
$380,000	$4,865.25	$3,910.94	$3,480.30	$3,254.26	$3,126.17
$390,000	$4,993.28	$4,013.85	$3,571.89	$3,339.89	$3,208.44
$400,000	$5,121.31	$4,116.77	$3,663.47	$3,425.53	$3,290.71

With an interest rate of 9.5%, your monthly payment will be:

Loan Amount	Number of Years in Term				
	10	15	20	25	30
$1,000	$12.54	$10.00	$8.84	$8.23	$7.87
$2,000	$25.07	$19.99	$17.68	$16.45	$15.74
$3,000	$37.60	$29.99	$26.52	$24.67	$23.61
$4,000	$50.14	$39.98	$35.35	$32.89	$31.47
$5,000	$62.67	$49.98	$44.19	$41.11	$39.34
$6,000	$75.20	$59.97	$53.03	$49.33	$47.21
$7,000	$87.73	$69.97	$61.86	$57.56	$55.07
$8,000	$100.27	$79.96	$70.70	$65.78	$62.94
$9,000	$112.80	$89.96	$79.54	$74.00	$70.81
$10,000	$125.33	$99.95	$88.38	$82.22	$78.68
$15,000	$188.00	$149.92	$132.56	$123.33	$118.01
$20,000	$250.66	$199.89	$176.75	$164.43	$157.35
$25,000	$313.32	$249.87	$220.93	$205.54	$196.68
$30,000	$375.99	$299.84	$265.12	$246.65	$236.02
$35,000	$438.65	$349.81	$309.30	$287.76	$275.35
$40,000	$501.31	$399.78	$353.49	$328.86	$314.69
$45,000	$563.98	$449.76	$397.67	$369.97	$354.02
$50,000	$626.64	$499.73	$441.86	$411.08	$393.36
$55,000	$689.30	$549.70	$486.05	$452.18	$432.69
$60,000	$751.97	$599.67	$530.23	$493.29	$472.03
$65,000	$814.63	$649.65	$574.42	$534.40	$511.36
$70,000	$877.29	$699.62	$618.60	$575.51	$550.70
$75,000	$939.96	$749.59	$662.79	$616.61	$590.03
$80,000	$1,002.62	$799.56	$706.97	$657.72	$629.37
$85,000	$1,065.28	$849.54	$751.16	$698.83	$668.70
$90,000	$1,127.95	$899.51	$795.34	$739.93	$708.04
$95,000	$1,190.61	$949.48	$839.53	$781.04	$747.37
$100,000	$1,253.27	$999.45	$883.72	$822.15	$786.71
$110,000	$1,378.60	$1,099.40	$972.09	$904.36	$865.38
$120,000	$1,503.93	$1,199.34	$1,060.46	$986.58	$944.05
$125,000	$1,566.59	$1,249.32	$1,104.64	$1,027.68	$983.38
$130,000	$1,629.25	$1,299.29	$1,148.83	$1,068.79	$1,022.72
$140,000	$1,754.58	$1,399.23	$1,237.20	$1,151.01	$1,101.39
$150,000	$1,879.91	$1,499.18	$1,325.57	$1,233.22	$1,180.06

With an interest rate of 9.5%, your monthly payment will be:

Loan Amount	Number of Years in Term				
	10	15	20	25	30
$160,000	$2,070.37	$1,670.76	$1,491.41	$1,397.92	$1,345.37
$170,000	$2,199.76	$1,775.19	$1,584.63	$1,485.29	$1,429.46
$175,000	$2,264.46	$1,827.40	$1,631.23	$1,528.97	$1,471.50
$180,000	$2,329.16	$1,879.61	$1,677.84	$1,572.66	$1,513.54
$190,000	$2,458.56	$1,984.03	$1,771.05	$1,660.03	$1,597.63
$200,000	$2,587.96	$2,088.45	$1,864.27	$1,747.40	$1,681.71
$210,000	$2,717.35	$2,192.88	$1,957.48	$1,834.77	$1,765.80
$220,000	$2,846.75	$2,297.30	$2,050.69	$1,922.14	$1,849.88
$225,000	$2,911.45	$2,349.51	$2,097.30	$1,965.82	$1,891.93
$230,000	$2,976.15	$2,401.72	$2,143.91	$2,009.51	$1,933.97
$240,000	$3,105.55	$2,506.14	$2,237.12	$2,096.88	$2,018.06
$250,000	$3,234.94	$2,610.57	$2,330.33	$2,184.25	$2,102.14
$260,000	$3,364.34	$2,714.99	$2,423.55	$2,271.62	$2,186.23
$270,000	$3,493.74	$2,819.41	$2,516.76	$2,358.99	$2,270.31
$275,000	$3,558.44	$2,871.62	$2,563.37	$2,402.67	$2,312.35
$280,000	$3,623.14	$2,923.83	$2,609.97	$2,446.36	$2,354.40
$290,000	$3,752.53	$3,028.26	$2,703.19	$2,533.73	$2,438.48
$300,000	$3,881.93	$3,132.68	$2,796.40	$2,621.09	$2,522.57
$310,000	$4,011.33	$3,237.10	$2,889.61	$2,708.46	$2,606.65
$320,000	$4,140.73	$3,341.52	$2,982.82	$2,795.83	$2,690.74
$325,000	$4,205.43	$3,393.74	$3,029.43	$2,839.52	$2,732.78
$330,000	$4,270.12	$3,445.95	$3,076.04	$2,883.20	$2,774.82
$340,000	$4,399.52	$3,550.37	$3,169.25	$2,970.57	$2,858.91
$350,000	$4,528.92	$3,654.79	$3,262.46	$3,057.94	$2,942.99
$360,000	$4,658.32	$3,759.21	$3,355.68	$3,145.31	$3,027.08
$370,000	$4,787.71	$3,863.64	$3,448.89	$3,232.68	$3,111.17
$375,000	$4,852.41	$3,915.85	$3,495.50	$3,276.37	$3,153.21
$380,000	$4,917.11	$3,968.06	$3,542.10	$3,320.05	$3,195.25
$390,000	$5,046.51	$4,072.48	$3,635.32	$3,407.42	$3,279.34
$400,000	$5,175.91	$4,176.90	$3,728.53	$3,494.79	$3,363.42

With an interest rate of 9.75%, your monthly payment will be:

Loan Amount	Number of Years in Term				
	10	15	20	25	30
$1,000	$13.08	$10.60	$9.49	$8.92	$8.60
$2,000	$26.16	$21.19	$18.98	$17.83	$17.19
$3,000	$39.24	$31.79	$28.46	$26.74	$25.78
$4,000	$52.31	$42.38	$37.95	$35.65	$34.37
$5,000	$65.39	$52.97	$47.43	$44.56	$42.96
$6,000	$78.47	$63.57	$56.92	$53.47	$51.55
$7,000	$91.54	$74.16	$66.40	$62.38	$60.15
$8,000	$104.62	$84.75	$75.89	$71.30	$68.74
$9,000	$117.70	$95.35	$85.37	$80.21	$77.33
$10,000	$130.78	$105.94	$94.86	$89.12	$85.92
$15,000	$196.16	$158.91	$142.28	$133.68	$128.88
$20,000	$261.55	$211.88	$189.71	$178.23	$171.84
$25,000	$326.93	$264.85	$237.13	$222.79	$214.79
$30,000	$392.32	$317.81	$284.56	$267.35	$257.75

With an interest rate of 9.75%, your monthly payment will be:

Loan Amount	Number of Years in Term				
	10	15	20	25	30
$35,000	$457.70	$370.78	$331.99	$311.90	$300.71
$40,000	$523.09	$423.75	$379.41	$356.46	$343.67
$45,000	$588.47	$476.72	$426.84	$401.02	$386.62
$50,000	$653.86	$529.69	$474.26	$445.57	$429.58
$55,000	$719.24	$582.65	$521.69	$490.13	$472.54
$60,000	$784.63	$635.62	$569.12	$534.69	$515.50
$65,000	$850.01	$688.59	$616.54	$579.24	$558.46
$70,000	$915.40	$741.56	$663.97	$623.80	$601.41
$75,000	$980.78	$794.53	$711.39	$668.36	$644.37
$80,000	$1,046.17	$847.50	$758.82	$712.91	$687.33
$85,000	$1,111.55	$900.46	$806.24	$757.47	$730.29
$90,000	$1,176.94	$953.43	$853.67	$802.03	$773.24
$95,000	$1,242.32	$1,006.40	$901.10	$846.59	$816.20
$100,000	$1,307.71	$1,059.37	$948.52	$891.14	$859.16
$110,000	$1,438.48	$1,165.30	$1,043.37	$980.26	$945.07
$120,000	$1,569.25	$1,271.24	$1,138.23	$1,069.37	$1,030.99
$125,000	$1,634.63	$1,324.21	$1,185.65	$1,113.93	$1,073.95
$130,000	$1,700.02	$1,377.18	$1,233.08	$1,158.48	$1,116.91
$140,000	$1,830.79	$1,483.11	$1,327.93	$1,247.60	$1,202.82
$150,000	$1,961.56	$1,589.05	$1,422.78	$1,336.71	$1,288.74
$160,000	$2,092.33	$1,694.99	$1,517.63	$1,425.82	$1,374.65
$170,000	$2,223.10	$1,800.92	$1,612.48	$1,514.94	$1,460.57
$175,000	$2,288.48	$1,853.89	$1,659.91	$1,559.50	$1,503.53
$180,000	$2,353.87	$1,906.86	$1,707.34	$1,604.05	$1,546.48
$190,000	$2,484.64	$2,012.79	$1,802.19	$1,693.17	$1,632.40
$200,000	$2,615.41	$2,118.73	$1,897.04	$1,782.28	$1,718.31
$210,000	$2,746.18	$2,224.67	$1,991.89	$1,871.39	$1,804.23
$220,000	$2,876.95	$2,330.60	$2,086.74	$1,960.51	$1,890.14
$225,000	$2,942.34	$2,383.57	$2,134.17	$2,005.06	$1,933.10
$230,000	$3,007.72	$2,436.54	$2,181.59	$2,049.62	$1,976.06
$240,000	$3,138.49	$2,542.48	$2,276.45	$2,138.73	$2,061.98
$250,000	$3,269.26	$2,648.41	$2,371.30	$2,227.85	$2,147.89
$260,000	$3,400.03	$2,754.35	$2,466.15	$2,316.96	$2,233.81
$270,000	$3,530.80	$2,860.28	$2,561.00	$2,406.08	$2,319.72
$275,000	$3,596.19	$2,913.25	$2,608.43	$2,450.63	$2,362.68
$280,000	$3,661.57	$2,966.22	$2,655.85	$2,495.19	$2,405.64
$290,000	$3,792.34	$3,072.16	$2,750.70	$2,584.30	$2,491.55
$300,000	$3,923.11	$3,178.09	$2,845.56	$2,673.42	$2,577.47
$310,000	$4,053.88	$3,284.03	$2,940.41	$2,762.53	$2,663.38
$320,000	$4,184.65	$3,389.97	$3,035.26	$2,851.64	$2,749.30
$325,000	$4,250.04	$3,442.93	$3,082.68	$2,896.20	$2,792.26
$330,000	$4,315.42	$3,495.90	$3,130.11	$2,940.76	$2,835.21
$340,000	$4,446.19	$3,601.84	$3,224.96	$3,029.87	$2,921.13
$350,000	$4,576.96	$3,707.77	$3,319.81	$3,118.99	$3,007.05
$360,000	$4,707.73	$3,813.71	$3,414.67	$3,208.10	$3,092.96
$370,000	$4,838.50	$3,919.65	$3,509.52	$3,297.21	$3,178.88
$375,000	$4,903.89	$3,972.61	$3,556.94	$3,341.77	$3,221.83
$380,000	$4,969.27	$4,025.58	$3,604.37	$3,386.33	$3,264.79
$390,000	$5,100.04	$4,131.52	$3,699.22	$3,475.44	$3,350.71
$400,000	$5,230.81	$4,237.46	$3,794.07	$3,564.55	$3,436.62

With an interest rate of 10.00%, your monthly payment will be:

Loan Amount	Number of Years in Term				
	10	15	20	25	30
$1,000	$13.22	$10.75	$9.66	$9.09	$8.78
$2,000	$26.44	$21.50	$19.31	$18.18	$17.56
$3,000	$39.65	$32.24	$28.96	$27.27	$26.33
$4,000	$52.87	$42.99	$38.61	$36.35	$35.11
$5,000	$66.08	$53.74	$48.26	$45.44	$43.88
$6,000	$79.30	$64.48	$57.91	$54.53	$52.66
$7,000	$92.51	$75.23	$67.56	$63.61	$61.44
$8,000	$105.73	$85.97	$77.21	$72.70	$70.21
$9,000	$118.94	$96.72	$86.86	$81.79	$78.99
$10,000	$132.16	$107.47	$96.51	$90.88	$87.76
$15,000	$198.23	$161.20	$144.76	$136.31	$131.64
$20,000	$264.31	$214.93	$193.01	$181.75	$175.52
$25,000	$330.38	$268.66	$241.26	$227.18	$219.40
$30,000	$396.46	$322.39	$289.51	$272.62	$263.28
$35,000	$462.53	$376.12	$337.76	$318.05	$307.16
$40,000	$528.61	$429.85	$386.01	$363.49	$351.03
$45,000	$594.68	$483.58	$434.26	$408.92	$394.91
$50,000	$660.76	$537.31	$482.52	$454.36	$438.79
$55,000	$726.83	$591.04	$530.77	$499.79	$482.67
$60,000	$792.91	$644.77	$579.02	$545.23	$526.55
$65,000	$858.98	$698.50	$627.27	$590.66	$570.43
$70,000	$925.06	$752.23	$675.52	$636.10	$614.31
$75,000	$991.14	$805.96	$723.77	$681.53	$658.18
$80,000	$1,057.21	$859.69	$772.02	$726.97	$702.06
$85,000	$1,123.29	$913.42	$820.27	$772.40	$745.94
$90,000	$1,189.36	$967.15	$868.52	$817.84	$789.82
$95,000	$1,255.44	$1,020.88	$916.78	$863.27	$833.70
$100,000	$1,321.51	$1,074.61	$965.03	$908.71	$877.58
$110,000	$1,453.66	$1,182.07	$1,061.53	$999.58	$965.33
$120,000	$1,585.81	$1,289.53	$1,158.03	$1,090.45	$1,053.09
$125,000	$1,651.89	$1,343.26	$1,206.28	$1,135.88	$1,096.97
$130,000	$1,717.96	$1,396.99	$1,254.53	$1,181.32	$1,140.85
$140,000	$1,850.12	$1,504.45	$1,351.04	$1,272.19	$1,228.61
$150,000	$1,982.27	$1,611.91	$1,447.54	$1,363.06	$1,316.36
$160,000	$2,114.42	$1,719.37	$1,544.04	$1,453.93	$1,404.12
$170,000	$2,246.57	$1,826.83	$1,640.54	$1,544.80	$1,491.88
$175,000	$2,312.64	$1,880.56	$1,688.79	$1,590.23	$1,535.76
$180,000	$2,378.72	$1,934.29	$1,737.04	$1,635.67	$1,579.63
$190,000	$2,510.87	$2,041.75	$1,833.55	$1,726.54	$1,667.39
$200,000	$2,643.02	$2,149.22	$1,930.05	$1,817.41	$1,755.15
$210,000	$2,775.17	$2,256.68	$2,026.55	$1,908.28	$1,842.91
$220,000	$2,907.32	$2,364.14	$2,123.05	$1,999.15	$1,930.66
$225,000	$2,973.40	$2,417.87	$2,171.30	$2,044.58	$1,974.54
$230,000	$3,039.47	$2,471.60	$2,219.55	$2,090.02	$2,018.42
$240,000	$3,171.62	$2,579.06	$2,316.06	$2,180.89	$2,106.18
$250,000	$3,303.77	$2,686.52	$2,412.56	$2,271.76	$2,193.93
$260,000	$3,435.92	$2,793.98	$2,509.06	$2,362.63	$2,281.69
$270,000	$3,568.07	$2,901.44	$2,605.56	$2,453.50	$2,369.45
$275,000	$3,634.15	$2,955.17	$2,653.81	$2,498.93	$2,413.33
$280,000	$3,700.23	$3,008.90	$2,702.07	$2,544.37	$2,457.21
$290,000	$3,832.38	$3,116.36	$2,798.57	$2,635.24	$2,544.96
$300,000	$3,964.53	$3,223.82	$2,895.07	$2,726.11	$2,632.72

With an interest rate of 10.00%, your monthly payment will be:

Loan Amount	Number of Years in Term				
	10	15	20	25	30
$310,000	$4,096.68	$3,331.28	$2,991.57	$2,816.98	$2,720.48
$320,000	$4,228.83	$3,438.74	$3,088.07	$2,907.85	$2,808.23
$325,000	$4,294.90	$3,492.47	$3,136.33	$2,953.28	$2,852.11
$330,000	$4,360.98	$3,546.20	$3,184.58	$2,998.72	$2,895.99
$340,000	$4,493.13	$3,653.66	$3,281.08	$3,089.59	$2,983.75
$350,000	$4,625.28	$3,761.12	$3,377.58	$3,180.46	$3,071.51
$360,000	$4,757.43	$3,868.58	$3,474.08	$3,271.33	$3,159.26
$370,000	$4,889.58	$3,976.04	$3,570.59	$3,362.20	$3,247.02
$375,000	$4,955.66	$4,029.77	$3,618.84	$3,407.63	$3,290.90
$380,000	$5,021.73	$4,083.50	$3,667.09	$3,453.07	$3,334.78
$390,000	$5,153.88	$4,190.96	$3,763.59	$3,543.94	$3,422.53
$400,000	$5,286.03	$4,298.43	$3,860.09	$3,634.81	$3,510.29

With an interest rate of 10.25%, your monthly payment will be:

Loan Amount	Number of Years in Term				
	10	15	20	25	30
$1,000	$13.36	$10.90	$9.82	$9.27	$8.97
$2,000	$26.71	$21.80	$19.64	$18.53	$17.93
$3,000	$40.07	$32.70	$29.45	$27.80	$26.89
$4,000	$53.42	$43.60	$39.27	$37.06	$35.85
$5,000	$66.77	$54.50	$49.09	$46.32	$44.81
$6,000	$80.13	$65.40	$58.90	$55.59	$53.77
$7,000	$93.48	$76.30	$68.72	$64.85	$62.73
$8,000	$106.84	$87.20	$78.54	$74.12	$71.69
$9,000	$120.19	$98.10	$88.35	$83.38	$80.65
$10,000	$133.54	$109.00	$98.17	$92.64	$89.62
$15,000	$200.31	$163.50	$147.25	$138.96	$134.42
$20,000	$267.08	$218.00	$196.33	$185.28	$179.23
$25,000	$333.85	$272.49	$245.42	$231.60	$224.03
$30,000	$400.62	$326.99	$294.50	$277.92	$268.84
$35,000	$467.39	$381.49	$343.58	$324.24	$313.64
$40,000	$534.16	$435.99	$392.66	$370.56	$358.45
$45,000	$600.93	$490.48	$441.74	$416.88	$403.25
$50,000	$667.70	$544.98	$490.83	$463.20	$448.06
$55,000	$734.47	$599.48	$539.91	$509.52	$492.86
$60,000	$801.24	$653.98	$588.99	$555.83	$537.67
$65,000	$868.01	$708.47	$638.07	$602.15	$582.47
$70,000	$934.78	$762.97	$687.16	$648.47	$627.28
$75,000	$1,001.55	$817.47	$736.24	$694.79	$672.08
$80,000	$1,068.32	$871.97	$785.32	$741.11	$716.89
$85,000	$1,135.09	$926.46	$834.40	$787.43	$761.69
$90,000	$1,201.86	$980.96	$883.48	$833.75	$806.50
$95,000	$1,268.63	$1,035.46	$932.57	$880.07	$851.30
$100,000	$1,335.40	$1,089.96	$981.65	$926.39	$896.11
$110,000	$1,468.93	$1,198.95	$1,079.81	$1,019.03	$985.72
$120,000	$1,602.47	$1,307.95	$1,177.98	$1,111.66	$1,075.33
$125,000	$1,669.24	$1,362.44	$1,227.06	$1,157.98	$1,120.13
$130,000	$1,736.01	$1,416.94	$1,276.14	$1,204.30	$1,164.94
$140,000	$1,869.55	$1,525.94	$1,374.31	$1,296.94	$1,254.55
$150,000	$2,003.09	$1,634.93	$1,472.47	$1,389.58	$1,344.16

With an interest rate of 10.25%, your monthly payment will be:

Loan Amount	Number of Years in Term				
	10	15	20	25	30
$160,000	$2,136.63	$1,743.93	$1,570.63	$1,482.22	$1,433.77
$170,000	$2,270.17	$1,852.92	$1,668.80	$1,574.86	$1,523.38
$175,000	$2,336.94	$1,907.42	$1,717.88	$1,621.18	$1,568.18
$180,000	$2,403.71	$1,961.92	$1,766.96	$1,667.49	$1,612.99
$190,000	$2,537.25	$2,070.91	$1,865.13	$1,760.13	$1,702.60
$200,000	$2,670.79	$2,179.91	$1,963.29	$1,852.77	$1,792.21
$210,000	$2,804.32	$2,288.90	$2,061.46	$1,945.41	$1,881.82
$220,000	$2,937.86	$2,397.90	$2,159.62	$2,038.05	$1,971.43
$225,000	$3,004.63	$2,452.39	$2,208.70	$2,084.37	$2,016.23
$230,000	$3,071.40	$2,506.89	$2,257.78	$2,130.69	$2,061.04
$240,000	$3,204.94	$2,615.89	$2,355.95	$2,223.32	$2,150.65
$250,000	$3,338.48	$2,724.88	$2,454.11	$2,315.96	$2,240.26
$260,000	$3,472.02	$2,833.88	$2,552.28	$2,408.60	$2,329.87
$270,000	$3,605.56	$2,942.87	$2,650.44	$2,501.24	$2,419.48
$275,000	$3,672.33	$2,997.37	$2,699.52	$2,547.56	$2,464.28
$280,000	$3,739.10	$3,051.87	$2,748.61	$2,593.88	$2,509.09
$290,000	$3,872.64	$3,160.86	$2,846.77	$2,686.52	$2,598.70
$300,000	$4,006.18	$3,269.86	$2,944.94	$2,779.15	$2,688.31
$310,000	$4,139.71	$3,378.85	$3,043.10	$2,871.79	$2,777.92
$320,000	$4,273.25	$3,487.85	$3,141.26	$2,964.43	$2,867.53
$325,000	$4,340.02	$3,542.35	$3,190.35	$3,010.75	$2,912.33
$330,000	$4,406.79	$3,596.84	$3,239.43	$3,057.07	$2,957.14
$340,000	$4,540.33	$3,705.84	$3,337.59	$3,149.71	$3,046.75
$350,000	$4,673.87	$3,814.83	$3,435.76	$3,242.35	$3,136.36
$360,000	$4,807.41	$3,923.83	$3,533.92	$3,334.98	$3,225.97
$370,000	$4,940.95	$4,032.82	$3,632.09	$3,427.62	$3,315.58
$375,000	$5,007.72	$4,087.32	$3,681.17	$3,473.94	$3,360.38
$380,000	$5,074.49	$4,141.82	$3,730.25	$3,520.26	$3,405.19
$390,000	$5,208.03	$4,250.81	$3,828.41	$3,612.90	$3,494.80
$400,000	$5,341.57	$4,359.81	$3,926.58	$3,705.54	$3,584.41

With an interest rate of 10.5%, your monthly payment will be:

Loan Amount	Number of Years in Term				
	10	15	20	25	30
$1,000	$13.50	$11.06	$9.99	$9.45	$9.15
$2,000	$26.99	$22.11	$19.97	$18.89	$18.30
$3,000	$40.49	$33.17	$29.96	$28.33	$27.45
$4,000	$53.98	$44.22	$39.94	$37.77	$36.59
$5,000	$67.47	$55.27	$49.92	$47.21	$45.74
$6,000	$80.97	$66.33	$59.91	$56.66	$54.89
$7,000	$94.46	$77.38	$69.89	$66.10	$64.04
$8,000	$107.95	$88.44	$79.88	$75.54	$73.18
$9,000	$121.45	$99.49	$89.86	$84.98	$82.33
$10,000	$134.94	$110.54	$99.84	$94.42	$91.48
$15,000	$202.41	$165.81	$149.76	$141.63	$137.22
$20,000	$269.87	$221.08	$199.68	$188.84	$182.95
$25,000	$337.34	$276.35	$249.60	$236.05	$228.69
$30,000	$404.81	$331.62	$299.52	$283.26	$274.43

With an interest rate of 10.5%, your monthly payment will be:

Loan Amount	Number of Years in Term				
	10	15	20	25	30
$35,000	$472.28	$386.89	$349.44	$330.47	$320.16
$40,000	$539.74	$442.16	$399.36	$377.68	$365.90
$45,000	$607.21	$497.43	$449.28	$424.89	$411.64
$50,000	$674.68	$552.70	$499.19	$472.10	$457.37
$55,000	$742.15	$607.97	$549.11	$519.30	$503.11
$60,000	$809.61	$663.24	$599.03	$566.51	$548.85
$65,000	$877.08	$718.51	$648.95	$613.72	$594.59
$70,000	$944.55	$773.78	$698.87	$660.93	$640.32
$75,000	$1,012.02	$829.05	$748.79	$708.14	$686.06
$80,000	$1,079.48	$884.32	$798.71	$755.35	$731.80
$85,000	$1,146.95	$939.59	$848.63	$802.56	$777.53
$90,000	$1,214.42	$994.86	$898.55	$849.77	$823.27
$95,000	$1,281.89	$1,050.13	$948.47	$896.98	$869.01
$100,000	$1,349.35	$1,105.40	$998.38	$944.19	$914.74
$110,000	$1,484.29	$1,215.94	$1,098.22	$1,038.60	$1,006.22
$120,000	$1,619.22	$1,326.48	$1,198.06	$1,133.02	$1,097.69
$125,000	$1,686.69	$1,381.75	$1,247.98	$1,180.23	$1,143.43
$130,000	$1,754.16	$1,437.02	$1,297.90	$1,227.44	$1,189.17
$140,000	$1,889.09	$1,547.56	$1,397.74	$1,321.86	$1,280.64
$150,000	$2,024.03	$1,658.10	$1,497.57	$1,416.28	$1,372.11
$160,000	$2,158.96	$1,768.64	$1,597.41	$1,510.70	$1,463.59
$170,000	$2,293.90	$1,879.18	$1,697.25	$1,605.11	$1,555.06
$175,000	$2,361.37	$1,934.45	$1,747.17	$1,652.32	$1,600.80
$180,000	$2,428.83	$1,989.72	$1,797.09	$1,699.53	$1,646.54
$190,000	$2,563.77	$2,100.26	$1,896.93	$1,793.95	$1,738.01
$200,000	$2,698.70	$2,210.80	$1,996.76	$1,888.37	$1,829.48
$210,000	$2,833.64	$2,321.34	$2,096.60	$1,982.79	$1,920.96
$220,000	$2,968.57	$2,431.88	$2,196.44	$2,077.20	$2,012.43
$225,000	$3,036.04	$2,487.15	$2,246.36	$2,124.41	$2,058.17
$230,000	$3,103.51	$2,542.42	$2,296.28	$2,171.62	$2,103.91
$240,000	$3,238.44	$2,652.96	$2,396.12	$2,266.04	$2,195.38
$250,000	$3,373.38	$2,763.50	$2,495.95	$2,360.46	$2,286.85
$260,000	$3,508.31	$2,874.04	$2,595.79	$2,454.88	$2,378.33
$270,000	$3,643.25	$2,984.58	$2,695.63	$2,549.30	$2,469.80
$275,000	$3,710.72	$3,039.85	$2,745.55	$2,596.50	$2,515.54
$280,000	$3,778.18	$3,095.12	$2,795.47	$2,643.71	$2,561.28
$290,000	$3,913.12	$3,205.66	$2,895.31	$2,738.13	$2,652.75
$300,000	$4,048.05	$3,316.20	$2,995.14	$2,832.55	$2,744.22
$310,000	$4,182.99	$3,426.74	$3,094.98	$2,926.97	$2,835.70
$320,000	$4,317.92	$3,537.28	$3,194.82	$3,021.39	$2,927.17
$325,000	$4,385.39	$3,592.55	$3,244.74	$3,068.60	$2,972.91
$330,000	$4,452.86	$3,647.82	$3,294.66	$3,115.80	$3,018.64
$340,000	$4,587.79	$3,758.36	$3,394.50	$3,210.22	$3,110.12
$350,000	$4,722.73	$3,868.90	$3,494.33	$3,304.64	$3,201.59
$360,000	$4,857.66	$3,979.44	$3,594.17	$3,399.06	$3,293.07
$370,000	$4,992.60	$4,089.98	$3,694.01	$3,493.48	$3,384.54
$375,000	$5,060.07	$4,145.25	$3,743.93	$3,540.69	$3,430.28
$380,000	$5,127.53	$4,200.52	$3,793.85	$3,587.90	$3,476.01
$390,000	$5,262.47	$4,311.06	$3,893.69	$3,682.31	$3,567.49
$400,000	$5,397.40	$4,421.60	$3,993.52	$3,776.73	$3,658.96

With an interest rate of 10.75%, your monthly payment will be:

Loan Amount	Number of Years in Term				
	10	15	20	25	30
$1,000	$13.64	$11.21	$10.16	$9.63	$9.34
$2,000	$27.27	$22.42	$20.31	$19.25	$18.67
$3,000	$40.91	$33.63	$30.46	$28.87	$28.01
$4,000	$54.54	$44.84	$40.61	$38.49	$37.34
$5,000	$68.17	$56.05	$50.77	$48.11	$46.68
$6,000	$81.81	$67.26	$60.92	$57.73	$56.01
$7,000	$95.44	$78.47	$71.07	$67.35	$65.35
$8,000	$109.08	$89.68	$81.22	$76.97	$74.68
$9,000	$122.71	$100.89	$91.38	$86.59	$84.02
$10,000	$136.34	$112.10	$101.53	$96.21	$93.35
$15,000	$204.51	$168.15	$152.29	$144.32	$140.03
$20,000	$272.68	$224.19	$203.05	$192.42	$186.70
$25,000	$340.85	$280.24	$253.81	$240.53	$233.38
$30,000	$409.02	$336.29	$304.57	$288.63	$280.05
$35,000	$477.19	$392.34	$355.34	$336.74	$326.72
$40,000	$545.36	$448.38	$406.10	$384.84	$373.40
$45,000	$613.53	$504.43	$456.86	$432.95	$420.07
$50,000	$681.70	$560.48	$507.62	$481.05	$466.75
$55,000	$749.87	$616.53	$558.38	$529.16	$513.42
$60,000	$818.04	$672.57	$609.14	$577.26	$560.09
$65,000	$886.21	$728.62	$659.90	$625.37	$606.77
$70,000	$954.38	$784.67	$710.67	$673.47	$653.44
$75,000	$1,022.55	$840.72	$761.43	$721.57	$700.12
$80,000	$1,090.71	$896.76	$812.19	$769.68	$746.79
$85,000	$1,158.88	$952.81	$862.95	$817.78	$793.46
$90,000	$1,227.05	$1,008.86	$913.71	$865.89	$840.14
$95,000	$1,295.22	$1,064.91	$964.47	$913.99	$886.81
$100,000	$1,363.39	$1,120.95	$1,015.23	$962.10	$933.49
$110,000	$1,499.73	$1,233.05	$1,116.76	$1,058.31	$1,026.83
$120,000	$1,636.07	$1,345.14	$1,218.28	$1,154.52	$1,120.18
$125,000	$1,704.24	$1,401.19	$1,269.04	$1,202.62	$1,166.86
$130,000	$1,772.41	$1,457.24	$1,319.80	$1,250.73	$1,213.53
$140,000	$1,908.75	$1,569.33	$1,421.33	$1,346.93	$1,306.88
$150,000	$2,045.09	$1,681.43	$1,522.85	$1,443.14	$1,400.23
$160,000	$2,181.42	$1,793.52	$1,624.37	$1,539.35	$1,493.58
$170,000	$2,317.76	$1,905.62	$1,725.89	$1,635.56	$1,586.92
$175,000	$2,385.93	$1,961.66	$1,776.66	$1,683.67	$1,633.60
$180,000	$2,454.10	$2,017.71	$1,827.42	$1,731.77	$1,680.27
$190,000	$2,590.44	$2,129.81	$1,928.94	$1,827.98	$1,773.62
$200,000	$2,726.78	$2,241.90	$2,030.46	$1,924.19	$1,866.97
$210,000	$2,863.12	$2,354.00	$2,131.99	$2,020.40	$1,960.32
$220,000	$2,999.46	$2,466.09	$2,233.51	$2,116.61	$2,053.66
$225,000	$3,067.63	$2,522.14	$2,284.27	$2,164.71	$2,100.34
$230,000	$3,135.79	$2,578.19	$2,335.03	$2,212.82	$2,147.01
$240,000	$3,272.13	$2,690.28	$2,436.55	$2,309.03	$2,240.36
$250,000	$3,408.47	$2,802.37	$2,538.08	$2,405.24	$2,333.71
$260,000	$3,544.81	$2,914.47	$2,639.60	$2,501.45	$2,427.06
$270,000	$3,681.15	$3,026.56	$2,741.12	$2,597.66	$2,520.40
$275,000	$3,749.32	$3,082.61	$2,791.88	$2,645.76	$2,567.08
$280,000	$3,817.49	$3,138.66	$2,842.65	$2,693.86	$2,613.75
$290,000	$3,953.83	$3,250.75	$2,944.17	$2,790.07	$2,707.10
$300,000	$4,090.17	$3,362.85	$3,045.69	$2,886.28	$2,800.45

With an interest rate of 10.75%, your monthly payment will be:

Loan Amount	Number of Years in Term				
	10	15	20	25	30
$310,000	$4,226.50	$3,474.94	$3,147.21	$2,982.49	$2,893.80
$320,000	$4,362.84	$3,587.04	$3,248.74	$3,078.70	$2,987.15
$325,000	$4,431.01	$3,643.09	$3,299.50	$3,126.81	$3,033.82
$330,000	$4,499.18	$3,699.13	$3,350.26	$3,174.91	$3,080.49
$340,000	$4,635.52	$3,811.23	$3,451.78	$3,271.12	$3,173.84
$350,000	$4,771.86	$3,923.32	$3,553.31	$3,367.33	$3,267.19
$360,000	$4,908.20	$4,035.42	$3,654.83	$3,463.54	$3,360.54
$370,000	$5,044.54	$4,147.51	$3,756.35	$3,559.75	$3,453.89
$375,000	$5,112.71	$4,203.56	$3,807.11	$3,607.85	$3,500.56
$380,000	$5,180.87	$4,259.61	$3,857.88	$3,655.96	$3,547.23
$390,000	$5,317.21	$4,371.70	$3,959.40	$3,752.17	$3,640.58
$400,000	$5,453.55	$4,483.80	$4,060.92	$3,848.38	$3,733.93

With an interest rate of 11.00%, your monthly payment will be:

Loan Amount	Number of Years in Term				
	10	15	20	25	30
$1,000	$13.78	$11.37	$10.33	$9.81	$9.53
$2,000	$27.56	$22.74	$20.65	$19.61	$19.05
$3,000	$41.33	$34.10	$30.97	$29.41	$28.57
$4,000	$55.11	$45.47	$41.29	$39.21	$38.10
$5,000	$68.88	$56.83	$51.61	$49.01	$47.62
$6,000	$82.66	$68.20	$61.94	$58.81	$57.14
$7,000	$96.43	$79.57	$72.26	$68.61	$66.67
$8,000	$110.21	$90.93	$82.58	$78.41	$76.19
$9,000	$123.98	$102.30	$92.90	$88.22	$85.71
$10,000	$137.76	$113.66	$103.22	$98.02	$95.24
$15,000	$206.63	$170.49	$154.83	$147.02	$142.85
$20,000	$275.51	$227.32	$206.44	$196.03	$190.47
$25,000	$344.38	$284.15	$258.05	$245.03	$238.09
$30,000	$413.26	$340.98	$309.66	$294.04	$285.70
$35,000	$482.13	$397.81	$361.27	$343.04	$333.32
$40,000	$551.01	$454.64	$412.88	$392.05	$380.93
$45,000	$619.88	$511.47	$464.49	$441.06	$428.55
$50,000	$688.76	$568.30	$516.10	$490.06	$476.17
$55,000	$757.63	$625.13	$567.71	$539.07	$523.78
$60,000	$826.51	$681.96	$619.32	$588.07	$571.40
$65,000	$895.38	$738.79	$670.93	$637.08	$619.02
$70,000	$964.26	$795.62	$722.54	$686.08	$666.63
$75,000	$1,033.13	$852.45	$774.15	$735.09	$714.25
$80,000	$1,102.01	$909.28	$825.76	$784.10	$761.86
$85,000	$1,170.88	$966.11	$877.37	$833.10	$809.48
$90,000	$1,239.76	$1,022.94	$928.97	$882.11	$857.10
$95,000	$1,308.63	$1,079.77	$980.58	$931.11	$904.71
$100,000	$1,377.51	$1,136.60	$1,032.19	$980.12	$952.33
$110,000	$1,515.26	$1,250.26	$1,135.41	$1,078.13	$1,047.56
$120,000	$1,653.01	$1,363.92	$1,238.63	$1,176.14	$1,142.79
$125,000	$1,721.88	$1,420.75	$1,290.24	$1,225.15	$1,190.41
$130,000	$1,790.76	$1,477.58	$1,341.85	$1,274.15	$1,238.03
$140,000	$1,928.51	$1,591.24	$1,445.07	$1,372.16	$1,333.26
$150,000	$2,066.26	$1,704.90	$1,548.29	$1,470.17	$1,428.49

With an interest rate of 11.00%, your monthly payment will be:

Loan Amount	Number of Years in Term				
	10	15	20	25	30
$160,000	$2,204.01	$1,818.56	$1,651.51	$1,568.19	$1,523.72
$170,000	$2,341.76	$1,932.22	$1,754.73	$1,666.20	$1,618.95
$175,000	$2,410.63	$1,989.05	$1,806.33	$1,715.20	$1,666.57
$180,000	$2,479.51	$2,045.88	$1,857.94	$1,764.21	$1,714.19
$190,000	$2,617.26	$2,159.54	$1,961.16	$1,862.22	$1,809.42
$200,000	$2,755.01	$2,273.20	$2,064.38	$1,960.23	$1,904.65
$210,000	$2,892.76	$2,386.86	$2,167.60	$2,058.24	$1,999.88
$220,000	$3,030.51	$2,500.52	$2,270.82	$2,156.25	$2,095.12
$225,000	$3,099.38	$2,557.35	$2,322.43	$2,205.26	$2,142.73
$230,000	$3,168.26	$2,614.18	$2,374.04	$2,254.27	$2,190.35
$240,000	$3,306.01	$2,727.84	$2,477.26	$2,352.28	$2,285.58
$250,000	$3,443.76	$2,841.50	$2,580.48	$2,450.29	$2,380.81
$260,000	$3,581.51	$2,955.16	$2,683.69	$2,548.30	$2,476.05
$270,000	$3,719.26	$3,068.82	$2,786.91	$2,646.31	$2,571.28
$275,000	$3,788.13	$3,125.65	$2,838.52	$2,695.32	$2,618.89
$280,000	$3,857.01	$3,182.48	$2,890.13	$2,744.32	$2,666.51
$290,000	$3,994.76	$3,296.14	$2,993.35	$2,842.33	$2,761.74
$300,000	$4,132.51	$3,409.80	$3,096.57	$2,940.34	$2,856.98
$310,000	$4,270.26	$3,523.46	$3,199.79	$3,038.36	$2,952.21
$320,000	$4,408.01	$3,637.12	$3,303.01	$3,136.37	$3,047.44
$325,000	$4,476.88	$3,693.95	$3,354.62	$3,185.37	$3,095.06
$330,000	$4,545.76	$3,750.77	$3,406.23	$3,234.38	$3,142.67
$340,000	$4,683.51	$3,864.43	$3,509.45	$3,332.39	$3,237.90
$350,000	$4,821.26	$3,978.09	$3,612.66	$3,430.40	$3,333.14
$360,000	$4,959.01	$4,091.75	$3,715.88	$3,528.41	$3,428.37
$370,000	$5,096.76	$4,205.41	$3,819.10	$3,626.42	$3,523.60
$375,000	$5,165.63	$4,262.24	$3,870.71	$3,675.43	$3,571.22
$380,000	$5,234.51	$4,319.07	$3,922.32	$3,724.43	$3,618.83
$390,000	$5,372.26	$4,432.73	$4,025.54	$3,822.45	$3,714.07
$400,000	$5,510.01	$4,546.39	$4,128.76	$3,920.46	$3,809.30

With an interest rate of 11.25%, your monthly payment will be:

Loan Amount	Number of Years in Term				
	10	15	20	25	30
$1,000	$13.92	$11.53	$10.50	$9.99	$9.72
$2,000	$27.84	$23.05	$20.99	$19.97	$19.43
$3,000	$41.76	$34.58	$31.48	$29.95	$29.14
$4,000	$55.67	$46.10	$41.98	$39.93	$38.86
$5,000	$69.59	$57.62	$52.47	$49.92	$48.57
$6,000	$83.51	$69.15	$62.96	$59.90	$58.28
$7,000	$97.42	$80.67	$73.45	$69.88	$67.99
$8,000	$111.34	$92.19	$83.95	$79.86	$77.71
$9,000	$125.26	$103.72	$94.44	$89.85	$87.42
$10,000	$139.17	$115.24	$104.93	$99.83	$97.13
$15,000	$208.76	$172.86	$157.39	$149.74	$145.69
$20,000	$278.34	$230.47	$209.86	$199.65	$194.26
$25,000	$347.93	$288.09	$262.32	$249.56	$242.82
$30,000	$417.51	$345.71	$314.78	$299.48	$291.38

With an interest rate of 11.25%, your monthly payment will be:

Loan Amount	Number of Years in Term				
	10	15	20	25	30
$35,000	$487.10	$403.33	$367.24	$349.39	$339.95
$40,000	$556.68	$460.94	$419.71	$399.30	$388.51
$45,000	$626.27	$518.56	$472.17	$449.21	$437.07
$50,000	$695.85	$576.18	$524.63	$499.12	$485.64
$55,000	$765.43	$633.79	$577.10	$549.04	$534.20
$60,000	$835.02	$691.41	$629.56	$598.95	$582.76
$65,000	$904.60	$749.03	$682.02	$648.86	$631.32
$70,000	$974.19	$806.65	$734.48	$698.77	$679.89
$75,000	$1,043.77	$864.26	$786.95	$748.68	$728.45
$80,000	$1,113.36	$921.88	$839.41	$798.60	$777.01
$85,000	$1,182.94	$979.50	$891.87	$848.51	$825.58
$90,000	$1,252.53	$1,037.12	$944.34	$898.42	$874.14
$95,000	$1,322.11	$1,094.73	$996.80	$948.33	$922.70
$100,000	$1,391.69	$1,152.35	$1,049.26	$998.24	$971.27
$110,000	$1,530.86	$1,267.58	$1,154.19	$1,098.07	$1,068.39
$120,000	$1,670.03	$1,382.82	$1,259.11	$1,197.89	$1,165.52
$125,000	$1,739.62	$1,440.44	$1,311.58	$1,247.80	$1,214.08
$130,000	$1,809.20	$1,498.05	$1,364.04	$1,297.72	$1,262.64
$140,000	$1,948.37	$1,613.29	$1,468.96	$1,397.54	$1,359.77
$150,000	$2,087.54	$1,728.52	$1,573.89	$1,497.36	$1,456.90
$160,000	$2,226.71	$1,843.76	$1,678.81	$1,597.19	$1,554.02
$170,000	$2,365.88	$1,958.99	$1,783.74	$1,697.01	$1,651.15
$175,000	$2,435.46	$2,016.61	$1,836.20	$1,746.92	$1,699.71
$180,000	$2,505.05	$2,074.23	$1,888.67	$1,796.84	$1,748.28
$190,000	$2,644.21	$2,189.46	$1,993.59	$1,896.66	$1,845.40
$200,000	$2,783.38	$2,304.69	$2,098.52	$1,996.48	$1,942.53
$210,000	$2,922.55	$2,419.93	$2,203.44	$2,096.31	$2,039.65
$220,000	$3,061.72	$2,535.16	$2,308.37	$2,196.13	$2,136.78
$225,000	$3,131.31	$2,592.78	$2,360.83	$2,246.04	$2,185.34
$230,000	$3,200.89	$2,650.40	$2,413.29	$2,295.96	$2,233.91
$240,000	$3,340.06	$2,765.63	$2,518.22	$2,395.78	$2,331.03
$250,000	$3,479.23	$2,880.87	$2,623.15	$2,495.60	$2,428.16
$260,000	$3,618.40	$2,996.10	$2,728.07	$2,595.43	$2,525.28
$270,000	$3,757.57	$3,111.34	$2,833.00	$2,695.25	$2,622.41
$275,000	$3,827.15	$3,168.95	$2,885.46	$2,745.16	$2,670.97
$280,000	$3,896.74	$3,226.57	$2,937.92	$2,795.08	$2,719.54
$290,000	$4,035.90	$3,341.80	$3,042.85	$2,894.90	$2,816.66
$300,000	$4,175.07	$3,457.04	$3,147.77	$2,994.72	$2,913.79
$310,000	$4,314.24	$3,572.27	$3,252.70	$3,094.55	$3,010.92
$320,000	$4,453.41	$3,687.51	$3,357.62	$3,194.37	$3,108.04
$325,000	$4,523.00	$3,745.12	$3,410.09	$3,244.28	$3,156.60
$330,000	$4,592.58	$3,802.74	$3,462.55	$3,294.20	$3,205.17
$340,000	$4,731.75	$3,917.98	$3,567.48	$3,394.02	$3,302.29
$350,000	$4,870.92	$4,033.21	$3,672.40	$3,493.84	$3,399.42
$360,000	$5,010.09	$4,148.45	$3,777.33	$3,593.67	$3,496.55
$370,000	$5,149.26	$4,263.68	$3,882.25	$3,693.49	$3,593.67
$375,000	$5,218.84	$4,321.30	$3,934.72	$3,743.40	$3,642.24
$380,000	$5,288.42	$4,378.91	$3,987.18	$3,793.32	$3,690.80
$390,000	$5,427.59	$4,494.15	$4,092.10	$3,893.14	$3,787.92
$400,000	$5,566.76	$4,609.38	$4,197.03	$3,992.96	$3,885.05

With an interest rate of 11.5%, your monthly payment will be:

Loan Amount	Number of Years in Term				
	10	15	20	25	30
$1,000	$14.06	$11.69	$10.67	$10.17	$9.91
$2,000	$28.12	$23.37	$21.33	$20.33	$19.81
$3,000	$42.18	$35.05	$32.00	$30.50	$29.71
$4,000	$56.24	$46.73	$42.66	$40.66	$39.62
$5,000	$70.30	$58.41	$53.33	$50.83	$49.52
$6,000	$84.36	$70.10	$63.99	$60.99	$59.42
$7,000	$98.42	$81.78	$74.66	$71.16	$69.33
$8,000	$112.48	$93.46	$85.32	$81.32	$79.23
$9,000	$126.54	$105.14	$95.98	$91.49	$89.13
$10,000	$140.60	$116.82	$106.65	$101.65	$99.03
$15,000	$210.90	$175.23	$159.97	$152.48	$148.55
$20,000	$281.20	$233.64	$213.29	$203.30	$198.06
$25,000	$351.49	$292.05	$266.61	$254.12	$247.58
$30,000	$421.79	$350.46	$319.93	$304.95	$297.09
$35,000	$492.09	$408.87	$373.26	$355.77	$346.61
$40,000	$562.39	$467.28	$426.58	$406.59	$396.12
$45,000	$632.68	$525.69	$479.90	$457.42	$445.64
$50,000	$702.98	$584.10	$533.22	$508.24	$495.15
$55,000	$773.28	$642.51	$586.54	$559.06	$544.67
$60,000	$843.58	$700.92	$639.86	$609.89	$594.18
$65,000	$913.88	$759.33	$693.18	$660.71	$643.69
$70,000	$984.17	$817.74	$746.51	$711.53	$693.21
$75,000	$1,054.47	$876.15	$799.83	$762.36	$742.72
$80,000	$1,124.77	$934.56	$853.15	$813.18	$792.24
$85,000	$1,195.07	$992.97	$906.47	$864.00	$841.75
$90,000	$1,265.36	$1,051.38	$959.79	$914.83	$891.27
$95,000	$1,335.66	$1,109.79	$1,013.11	$965.65	$940.78
$100,000	$1,405.96	$1,168.19	$1,066.43	$1,016.47	$990.30
$110,000	$1,546.55	$1,285.01	$1,173.08	$1,118.12	$1,089.33
$120,000	$1,687.15	$1,401.83	$1,279.72	$1,219.77	$1,188.35
$125,000	$1,757.45	$1,460.24	$1,333.04	$1,270.59	$1,237.87
$130,000	$1,827.75	$1,518.65	$1,386.36	$1,321.41	$1,287.38
$140,000	$1,968.34	$1,635.47	$1,493.01	$1,423.06	$1,386.41
$150,000	$2,108.94	$1,752.29	$1,599.65	$1,524.71	$1,485.44
$160,000	$2,249.53	$1,869.11	$1,706.29	$1,626.36	$1,584.47
$170,000	$2,390.13	$1,985.93	$1,812.94	$1,728.00	$1,683.50
$175,000	$2,460.43	$2,044.34	$1,866.26	$1,778.83	$1,733.02
$180,000	$2,530.72	$2,102.75	$1,919.58	$1,829.65	$1,782.53
$190,000	$2,671.32	$2,219.57	$2,026.22	$1,931.30	$1,881.56
$200,000	$2,811.91	$2,336.38	$2,132.86	$2,032.94	$1,980.59
$210,000	$2,952.51	$2,453.20	$2,239.51	$2,134.59	$2,079.62
$220,000	$3,093.10	$2,570.02	$2,346.15	$2,236.24	$2,178.65
$225,000	$3,163.40	$2,628.43	$2,399.47	$2,287.06	$2,228.16
$230,000	$3,233.70	$2,686.84	$2,452.79	$2,337.88	$2,277.68
$240,000	$3,374.30	$2,803.66	$2,559.44	$2,439.53	$2,376.70
$250,000	$3,514.89	$2,920.48	$2,666.08	$2,541.18	$2,475.73
$260,000	$3,655.49	$3,037.30	$2,772.72	$2,642.82	$2,574.76
$270,000	$3,796.08	$3,154.12	$2,879.37	$2,744.47	$2,673.79
$275,000	$3,866.38	$3,212.53	$2,932.69	$2,795.29	$2,723.31
$280,000	$3,936.68	$3,270.94	$2,986.01	$2,846.12	$2,772.82
$290,000	$4,077.27	$3,387.76	$3,092.65	$2,947.76	$2,871.85
$300,000	$4,217.87	$3,504.57	$3,199.29	$3,049.41	$2,970.88

With an interest rate of 11.5%, your monthly payment will be:

Loan Amount	Number of Years in Term				
	10	15	20	25	30
$310,000	$4,358.46	$3,621.39	$3,305.94	$3,151.06	$3,069.91
$320,000	$4,499.06	$3,738.21	$3,412.58	$3,252.71	$3,168.94
$325,000	$4,569.36	$3,796.62	$3,465.90	$3,303.53	$3,218.45
$330,000	$4,639.65	$3,855.03	$3,519.22	$3,354.35	$3,267.97
$340,000	$4,780.25	$3,971.85	$3,625.87	$3,456.00	$3,367.00
$350,000	$4,920.85	$4,088.67	$3,732.51	$3,557.65	$3,466.03
$360,000	$5,061.44	$4,205.49	$3,839.15	$3,659.29	$3,565.05
$370,000	$5,202.04	$4,322.31	$3,945.79	$3,760.94	$3,664.08
$375,000	$5,272.33	$4,380.72	$3,999.12	$3,811.76	$3,713.60
$380,000	$5,342.63	$4,439.13	$4,052.44	$3,862.59	$3,763.11
$390,000	$5,483.23	$4,555.95	$4,159.08	$3,964.23	$3,862.14
$400,000	$5,623.82	$4,672.76	$4,265.72	$4,065.88	$3,961.17

With an interest rate of 11.75%, your monthly payment will be:

Loan Amount	Number of Years in Term				
	10	15	20	25	30
$1,000	$14.21	$11.85	$10.84	$10.35	$10.10
$2,000	$28.41	$23.69	$21.68	$20.70	$20.19
$3,000	$42.61	$35.53	$32.52	$31.05	$30.29
$4,000	$56.82	$47.37	$43.35	$41.40	$40.38
$5,000	$71.02	$59.21	$54.19	$51.74	$50.48
$6,000	$85.22	$71.05	$65.03	$62.09	$60.57
$7,000	$99.43	$82.89	$75.86	$72.44	$70.66
$8,000	$113.63	$94.74	$86.70	$82.79	$80.76
$9,000	$127.83	$106.58	$97.54	$93.14	$90.85
$10,000	$142.03	$118.42	$108.38	$103.48	$100.95
$15,000	$213.05	$177.62	$162.56	$155.22	$151.42
$20,000	$284.06	$236.83	$216.75	$206.96	$201.89
$25,000	$355.08	$296.04	$270.93	$258.70	$252.36
$30,000	$426.09	$355.24	$325.12	$310.44	$302.83
$35,000	$497.11	$414.45	$379.30	$362.18	$353.30
$40,000	$568.12	$473.66	$433.49	$413.92	$403.77
$45,000	$639.14	$532.86	$487.67	$465.66	$454.24
$50,000	$710.15	$592.07	$541.86	$517.40	$504.71
$55,000	$781.17	$651.28	$596.04	$569.14	$555.18
$60,000	$852.18	$710.48	$650.23	$620.88	$605.65
$65,000	$923.20	$769.69	$704.41	$672.62	$656.12
$70,000	$994.21	$828.90	$758.60	$724.36	$706.59
$75,000	$1,065.23	$888.10	$812.79	$776.10	$757.06
$80,000	$1,136.24	$947.31	$866.97	$827.84	$807.53
$85,000	$1,207.26	$1,006.52	$921.16	$879.58	$858.00
$90,000	$1,278.27	$1,065.72	$975.34	$931.32	$908.47
$95,000	$1,349.28	$1,124.93	$1,029.53	$983.06	$958.94
$100,000	$1,420.30	$1,184.14	$1,083.71	$1,034.80	$1,009.41
$110,000	$1,562.33	$1,302.55	$1,192.08	$1,138.28	$1,110.36
$120,000	$1,704.36	$1,420.96	$1,300.45	$1,241.76	$1,211.30
$125,000	$1,775.37	$1,480.17	$1,354.64	$1,293.50	$1,261.77
$130,000	$1,846.39	$1,539.38	$1,408.82	$1,345.24	$1,312.24
$140,000	$1,988.42	$1,657.79	$1,517.19	$1,448.72	$1,413.18
$150,000	$2,130.45	$1,776.20	$1,625.57	$1,552.20	$1,514.12

With an interest rate of 11.75%, your monthly payment will be:

Loan Amount	Number of Years in Term				
	10	15	20	25	30
$160,000	$2,272.48	$1,894.62	$1,733.94	$1,655.68	$1,615.06
$170,000	$2,414.51	$2,013.03	$1,842.31	$1,759.16	$1,716.00
$175,000	$2,485.52	$2,072.23	$1,896.49	$1,810.90	$1,766.47
$180,000	$2,556.54	$2,131.44	$1,950.68	$1,862.64	$1,816.94
$190,000	$2,698.56	$2,249.85	$2,059.05	$1,966.12	$1,917.88
$200,000	$2,840.59	$2,368.27	$2,167.42	$2,069.60	$2,018.82
$210,000	$2,982.62	$2,486.68	$2,275.79	$2,173.08	$2,119.77
$220,000	$3,124.65	$2,605.09	$2,384.16	$2,276.56	$2,220.71
$225,000	$3,195.67	$2,664.30	$2,438.35	$2,328.30	$2,271.18
$230,000	$3,266.68	$2,723.51	$2,492.53	$2,380.04	$2,321.65
$240,000	$3,408.71	$2,841.92	$2,600.90	$2,483.52	$2,422.59
$250,000	$3,550.74	$2,960.33	$2,709.27	$2,587.00	$2,523.53
$260,000	$3,692.77	$3,078.75	$2,817.64	$2,690.48	$2,624.47
$270,000	$3,834.80	$3,197.16	$2,926.01	$2,793.96	$2,725.41
$275,000	$3,905.82	$3,256.37	$2,980.20	$2,845.70	$2,775.88
$280,000	$3,976.83	$3,315.57	$3,034.38	$2,897.44	$2,826.35
$290,000	$4,118.86	$3,433.99	$3,142.76	$3,000.92	$2,927.29
$300,000	$4,260.89	$3,552.40	$3,251.13	$3,104.40	$3,028.23
$310,000	$4,402.92	$3,670.81	$3,359.50	$3,207.88	$3,129.18
$320,000	$4,544.95	$3,789.23	$3,467.87	$3,311.36	$3,230.12
$325,000	$4,615.96	$3,848.43	$3,522.05	$3,363.10	$3,280.59
$330,000	$4,686.98	$3,907.64	$3,576.24	$3,414.84	$3,331.06
$340,000	$4,829.01	$4,026.05	$3,684.61	$3,518.32	$3,432.00
$350,000	$4,971.04	$4,144.46	$3,792.98	$3,621.80	$3,532.94
$360,000	$5,113.07	$4,262.88	$3,901.35	$3,725.28	$3,633.88
$370,000	$5,255.09	$4,381.29	$4,009.72	$3,828.76	$3,734.82
$375,000	$5,326.11	$4,440.50	$4,063.91	$3,880.50	$3,785.29
$380,000	$5,397.12	$4,499.70	$4,118.09	$3,932.24	$3,835.76
$390,000	$5,539.15	$4,618.12	$4,226.46	$4,035.72	$3,936.70
$400,000	$5,681.18	$4,736.53	$4,334.83	$4,139.20	$4,037.64

With an interest rate of 12.00%, your monthly payment will be:

Loan Amount	Number of Years in Term				
	10	15	20	25	30
$1,000	$14.35	$12.01	$11.02	$10.54	$10.29
$2,000	$28.70	$24.01	$22.03	$21.07	$20.58
$3,000	$43.05	$36.01	$33.04	$31.60	$30.86
$4,000	$57.39	$48.01	$44.05	$42.13	$41.15
$5,000	$71.74	$60.01	$55.06	$52.67	$51.44
$6,000	$86.09	$72.02	$66.07	$63.20	$61.72
$7,000	$100.43	$84.02	$77.08	$73.73	$72.01
$8,000	$114.78	$96.02	$88.09	$84.26	$82.29
$9,000	$129.13	$108.02	$99.10	$94.80	$92.58
$10,000	$143.48	$120.02	$110.11	$105.33	$102.87
$15,000	$215.21	$180.03	$165.17	$157.99	$154.30
$20,000	$286.95	$240.04	$220.22	$210.65	$205.73
$25,000	$358.68	$300.05	$275.28	$263.31	$257.16
$30,000	$430.42	$360.06	$330.33	$315.97	$308.59

With an interest rate of 12.00%, your monthly payment will be:

Loan Amount	Number of Years in Term				
	10	15	20	25	30
$35,000	$502.15	$420.06	$385.39	$368.63	$360.02
$40,000	$573.89	$480.07	$440.44	$421.29	$411.45
$45,000	$645.62	$540.08	$495.49	$473.96	$462.88
$50,000	$717.36	$600.09	$550.55	$526.62	$514.31
$55,000	$789.10	$660.10	$605.60	$579.28	$565.74
$60,000	$860.83	$720.11	$660.66	$631.94	$617.17
$65,000	$932.57	$780.11	$715.71	$684.60	$668.60
$70,000	$1,004.30	$840.12	$770.77	$737.26	$720.03
$75,000	$1,076.04	$900.13	$825.82	$789.92	$771.46
$80,000	$1,147.77	$960.14	$880.87	$842.58	$822.90
$85,000	$1,219.51	$1,020.15	$935.93	$895.25	$874.33
$90,000	$1,291.24	$1,080.16	$990.98	$947.91	$925.76
$95,000	$1,362.98	$1,140.16	$1,046.04	$1,000.57	$977.19
$100,000	$1,434.71	$1,200.17	$1,101.09	$1,053.23	$1,028.62
$110,000	$1,578.19	$1,320.19	$1,211.20	$1,158.55	$1,131.48
$120,000	$1,721.66	$1,440.21	$1,321.31	$1,263.87	$1,234.34
$125,000	$1,793.39	$1,500.22	$1,376.36	$1,316.54	$1,285.77
$130,000	$1,865.13	$1,560.22	$1,431.42	$1,369.20	$1,337.20
$140,000	$2,008.60	$1,680.24	$1,541.53	$1,474.52	$1,440.06
$150,000	$2,152.07	$1,800.26	$1,651.63	$1,579.84	$1,542.92
$160,000	$2,295.54	$1,920.27	$1,761.74	$1,685.16	$1,645.79
$170,000	$2,439.01	$2,040.29	$1,871.85	$1,790.49	$1,748.65
$175,000	$2,510.75	$2,100.30	$1,926.91	$1,843.15	$1,800.08
$180,000	$2,582.48	$2,160.31	$1,981.96	$1,895.81	$1,851.51
$190,000	$2,725.95	$2,280.32	$2,092.07	$2,001.13	$1,954.37
$200,000	$2,869.42	$2,400.34	$2,202.18	$2,106.45	$2,057.23
$210,000	$3,012.89	$2,520.36	$2,312.29	$2,211.78	$2,160.09
$220,000	$3,156.37	$2,640.37	$2,422.39	$2,317.10	$2,262.95
$225,000	$3,228.10	$2,700.38	$2,477.45	$2,369.76	$2,314.38
$230,000	$3,299.84	$2,760.39	$2,532.50	$2,422.42	$2,365.81
$240,000	$3,443.31	$2,880.41	$2,642.61	$2,527.74	$2,468.68
$250,000	$3,586.78	$3,000.43	$2,752.72	$2,633.07	$2,571.54
$260,000	$3,730.25	$3,120.44	$2,862.83	$2,738.39	$2,674.40
$270,000	$3,873.72	$3,240.46	$2,972.94	$2,843.71	$2,777.26
$275,000	$3,945.46	$3,300.47	$3,027.99	$2,896.37	$2,828.69
$280,000	$4,017.19	$3,360.48	$3,083.05	$2,949.03	$2,880.12
$290,000	$4,160.66	$3,480.49	$3,193.15	$3,054.36	$2,982.98
$300,000	$4,304.13	$3,600.51	$3,303.26	$3,159.68	$3,085.84
$310,000	$4,447.60	$3,720.53	$3,413.37	$3,265.00	$3,188.70
$320,000	$4,591.08	$3,840.54	$3,523.48	$3,370.32	$3,291.57
$325,000	$4,662.81	$3,900.55	$3,578.53	$3,422.98	$3,343.00
$330,000	$4,734.55	$3,960.56	$3,633.59	$3,475.64	$3,394.43
$340,000	$4,878.02	$4,080.58	$3,743.70	$3,580.97	$3,497.29
$350,000	$5,021.49	$4,200.59	$3,853.81	$3,686.29	$3,600.15
$360,000	$5,164.96	$4,320.61	$3,963.92	$3,791.61	$3,703.01
$370,000	$5,308.43	$4,440.63	$4,074.02	$3,896.93	$3,805.87
$375,000	$5,380.17	$4,500.64	$4,129.08	$3,949.60	$3,857.30
$380,000	$5,451.90	$4,560.64	$4,184.13	$4,002.26	$3,908.73
$390,000	$5,595.37	$4,680.66	$4,294.24	$4,107.58	$4,011.59
$400,000	$5,738.84	$4,800.68	$4,404.35	$4,212.90	$4,114.46

With an interest rate of 12.25%, your monthly payment will be:

Loan Amount	Number of Years in Term				
	10	15	20	25	30
$1,000	$14.50	$12.17	$11.19	$10.72	$10.48
$2,000	$28.99	$24.33	$22.38	$21.44	$20.96
$3,000	$43.48	$36.49	$33.56	$32.16	$31.44
$4,000	$57.97	$48.66	$44.75	$42.87	$41.92
$5,000	$72.46	$60.82	$55.93	$53.59	$52.40
$6,000	$86.96	$72.98	$67.12	$64.31	$62.88
$7,000	$101.45	$85.15	$78.30	$75.03	$73.36
$8,000	$115.94	$97.31	$89.49	$85.74	$83.84
$9,000	$130.43	$109.47	$100.68	$96.46	$94.32
$10,000	$144.92	$121.63	$111.86	$107.18	$104.79
$15,000	$217.38	$182.45	$167.79	$160.77	$157.19
$20,000	$289.84	$243.26	$223.72	$214.35	$209.58
$25,000	$362.30	$304.08	$279.65	$267.94	$261.98
$30,000	$434.76	$364.89	$335.57	$321.53	$314.37
$35,000	$507.22	$425.71	$391.50	$375.12	$366.77
$40,000	$579.68	$486.52	$447.43	$428.70	$419.16
$45,000	$652.14	$547.34	$503.36	$482.29	$471.56
$50,000	$724.60	$608.15	$559.29	$535.88	$523.95
$55,000	$797.06	$668.97	$615.22	$589.46	$576.35
$60,000	$869.52	$729.78	$671.14	$643.05	$628.74
$65,000	$941.98	$790.60	$727.07	$696.64	$681.14
$70,000	$1,014.44	$851.41	$783.00	$750.23	$733.53
$75,000	$1,086.90	$912.23	$838.93	$803.81	$785.93
$80,000	$1,159.36	$973.04	$894.86	$857.40	$838.32
$85,000	$1,231.82	$1,033.86	$950.78	$910.99	$890.72
$90,000	$1,304.28	$1,094.67	$1,006.71	$964.57	$943.11
$95,000	$1,376.74	$1,155.49	$1,062.64	$1,018.16	$995.51
$100,000	$1,449.20	$1,216.30	$1,118.57	$1,071.75	$1,047.90
$110,000	$1,594.12	$1,337.93	$1,230.43	$1,178.92	$1,152.69
$120,000	$1,739.04	$1,459.56	$1,342.28	$1,286.10	$1,257.48
$125,000	$1,811.50	$1,520.38	$1,398.21	$1,339.68	$1,309.88
$130,000	$1,883.96	$1,581.19	$1,454.14	$1,393.27	$1,362.27
$140,000	$2,028.88	$1,702.82	$1,566.00	$1,500.45	$1,467.06
$150,000	$2,173.80	$1,824.45	$1,677.85	$1,607.62	$1,571.85
$160,000	$2,318.72	$1,946.08	$1,789.71	$1,714.80	$1,676.64
$170,000	$2,463.64	$2,067.71	$1,901.56	$1,821.97	$1,781.43
$175,000	$2,536.10	$2,128.53	$1,957.49	$1,875.56	$1,833.82
$180,000	$2,608.56	$2,189.34	$2,013.42	$1,929.14	$1,886.22
$190,000	$2,753.48	$2,310.97	$2,125.28	$2,036.32	$1,991.01
$200,000	$2,898.40	$2,432.60	$2,237.13	$2,143.49	$2,095.80
$210,000	$3,043.32	$2,554.23	$2,348.99	$2,250.67	$2,200.59
$220,000	$3,188.24	$2,675.86	$2,460.85	$2,357.84	$2,305.38
$225,000	$3,260.70	$2,736.68	$2,516.78	$2,411.43	$2,357.77
$230,000	$3,333.16	$2,797.49	$2,572.70	$2,465.02	$2,410.17
$240,000	$3,478.08	$2,919.12	$2,684.56	$2,572.19	$2,514.96
$250,000	$3,623.00	$3,040.75	$2,796.42	$2,679.36	$2,619.75
$260,000	$3,767.92	$3,162.38	$2,908.27	$2,786.54	$2,724.54
$270,000	$3,912.84	$3,284.01	$3,020.13	$2,893.71	$2,829.33
$275,000	$3,985.30	$3,344.83	$3,076.06	$2,947.30	$2,881.72
$280,000	$4,057.76	$3,405.64	$3,131.99	$3,000.89	$2,934.12
$290,000	$4,202.68	$3,527.27	$3,243.84	$3,108.06	$3,038.90
$300,000	$4,347.60	$3,648.90	$3,355.70	$3,215.24	$3,143.69

With an interest rate of 12.25%, your monthly payment will be:

Loan Amount	Number of Years in Term				
	10	15	20	25	30
$310,000	$4,492.52	$3,770.53	$3,467.56	$3,322.41	$3,248.48
$320,000	$4,637.44	$3,892.16	$3,579.41	$3,429.59	$3,353.27
$325,000	$4,709.90	$3,952.98	$3,635.34	$3,483.17	$3,405.67
$330,000	$4,782.36	$4,013.79	$3,691.27	$3,536.76	$3,458.06
$340,000	$4,927.28	$4,135.42	$3,803.12	$3,643.93	$3,562.85
$350,000	$5,072.20	$4,257.05	$3,914.98	$3,751.11	$3,667.64
$360,000	$5,217.12	$4,378.68	$4,026.84	$3,858.28	$3,772.43
$370,000	$5,362.04	$4,500.31	$4,138.69	$3,965.46	$3,877.22
$375,000	$5,434.50	$4,561.13	$4,194.62	$4,019.04	$3,929.62
$380,000	$5,506.96	$4,621.94	$4,250.55	$4,072.63	$3,982.01
$390,000	$5,651.88	$4,743.57	$4,362.41	$4,179.81	$4,086.80
$400,000	$5,796.80	$4,865.20	$4,474.26	$4,286.98	$4,191.59

With an interest rate of 12.5%, your monthly payment will be:

Loan Amount	Number of Years in Term				
	10	15	20	25	30
$1,000	$14.64	$12.33	$11.37	$10.91	$10.68
$2,000	$29.28	$24.66	$22.73	$21.81	$21.35
$3,000	$43.92	$36.98	$34.09	$32.72	$32.02
$4,000	$58.56	$49.31	$45.45	$43.62	$42.70
$5,000	$73.19	$61.63	$56.81	$54.52	$53.37
$6,000	$87.83	$73.96	$68.17	$65.43	$64.04
$7,000	$102.47	$86.28	$79.53	$76.33	$74.71
$8,000	$117.11	$98.61	$90.90	$87.23	$85.39
$9,000	$131.74	$110.93	$102.26	$98.14	$96.06
$10,000	$146.38	$123.26	$113.62	$109.04	$106.73
$15,000	$219.57	$184.88	$170.43	$163.56	$160.09
$20,000	$292.76	$246.51	$227.23	$218.08	$213.46
$25,000	$365.95	$308.14	$284.04	$272.59	$266.82
$30,000	$439.13	$369.76	$340.85	$327.11	$320.18
$35,000	$512.32	$431.39	$397.65	$381.63	$373.55
$40,000	$585.51	$493.01	$454.46	$436.15	$426.91
$45,000	$658.70	$554.64	$511.27	$490.66	$480.27
$50,000	$731.89	$616.27	$568.08	$545.18	$533.63
$55,000	$805.07	$677.89	$624.88	$599.70	$587.00
$60,000	$878.26	$739.52	$681.69	$654.22	$640.36
$65,000	$951.45	$801.14	$738.50	$708.74	$693.72
$70,000	$1,024.64	$862.77	$795.30	$763.25	$747.09
$75,000	$1,097.83	$924.40	$852.11	$817.77	$800.45
$80,000	$1,171.01	$986.02	$908.92	$872.29	$853.81
$85,000	$1,244.20	$1,047.65	$965.72	$926.81	$907.17
$90,000	$1,317.39	$1,109.27	$1,022.53	$981.32	$960.54
$95,000	$1,390.58	$1,170.90	$1,079.34	$1,035.84	$1,013.90
$100,000	$1,463.77	$1,232.53	$1,136.15	$1,090.36	$1,067.26
$110,000	$1,610.14	$1,355.78	$1,249.76	$1,199.39	$1,173.99
$120,000	$1,756.52	$1,479.03	$1,363.37	$1,308.43	$1,280.71
$125,000	$1,829.71	$1,540.66	$1,420.18	$1,362.95	$1,334.08
$130,000	$1,902.90	$1,602.28	$1,476.99	$1,417.47	$1,387.44
$140,000	$2,049.27	$1,725.54	$1,590.60	$1,526.50	$1,494.17
$150,000	$2,195.65	$1,848.79	$1,704.22	$1,635.54	$1,600.89

With an interest rate of 12.5%, your monthly payment will be:

Loan Amount	Number of Years in Term				
	10	15	20	25	30
$160,000	$2,342.02	$1,972.04	$1,817.83	$1,744.57	$1,707.62
$170,000	$2,488.40	$2,095.29	$1,931.44	$1,853.61	$1,814.34
$175,000	$2,561.59	$2,156.92	$1,988.25	$1,908.12	$1,867.71
$180,000	$2,634.78	$2,218.54	$2,045.06	$1,962.64	$1,921.07
$190,000	$2,781.15	$2,341.80	$2,158.67	$2,071.68	$2,027.79
$200,000	$2,927.53	$2,465.05	$2,272.29	$2,180.71	$2,134.52
$210,000	$3,073.90	$2,588.30	$2,385.90	$2,289.75	$2,241.25
$220,000	$3,220.28	$2,711.55	$2,499.51	$2,398.78	$2,347.97
$225,000	$3,293.47	$2,773.18	$2,556.32	$2,453.30	$2,401.33
$230,000	$3,366.66	$2,834.81	$2,613.13	$2,507.82	$2,454.70
$240,000	$3,513.03	$2,958.06	$2,726.74	$2,616.85	$2,561.42
$250,000	$3,659.41	$3,081.31	$2,840.36	$2,725.89	$2,668.15
$260,000	$3,805.79	$3,204.56	$2,953.97	$2,834.93	$2,774.88
$270,000	$3,952.16	$3,327.81	$3,067.58	$2,943.96	$2,881.60
$275,000	$4,025.35	$3,389.44	$3,124.39	$2,998.48	$2,934.96
$280,000	$4,098.54	$3,451.07	$3,181.20	$3,053.00	$2,988.33
$290,000	$4,244.91	$3,574.32	$3,294.81	$3,162.03	$3,095.05
$300,000	$4,391.29	$3,697.57	$3,408.43	$3,271.07	$3,201.78
$310,000	$4,537.67	$3,820.82	$3,522.04	$3,380.10	$3,308.50
$320,000	$4,684.04	$3,944.08	$3,635.65	$3,489.14	$3,415.23
$325,000	$4,757.23	$4,005.70	$3,692.46	$3,543.66	$3,468.59
$330,000	$4,830.42	$4,067.33	$3,749.27	$3,598.17	$3,521.96
$340,000	$4,976.79	$4,190.58	$3,862.88	$3,707.21	$3,628.68
$350,000	$5,123.17	$4,313.83	$3,976.50	$3,816.24	$3,735.41
$360,000	$5,269.55	$4,437.08	$4,090.11	$3,925.28	$3,842.13
$370,000	$5,415.92	$4,560.34	$4,203.73	$4,034.32	$3,948.86
$375,000	$5,489.11	$4,621.96	$4,260.53	$4,088.83	$4,002.22
$380,000	$5,562.30	$4,683.59	$4,317.34	$4,143.35	$4,055.58
$390,000	$5,708.68	$4,806.84	$4,430.95	$4,252.39	$4,162.31
$400,000	$5,855.05	$4,930.09	$4,544.57	$4,361.42	$4,269.04

With an interest rate of 12.75%, your monthly payment will be:

Loan Amount	Number of Years in Term				
	10	15	20	25	30
$1,000	$14.79	$12.49	$11.54	$11.10	$10.87
$2,000	$29.57	$24.98	$23.08	$22.19	$21.74
$3,000	$44.36	$37.47	$34.62	$33.28	$32.61
$4,000	$59.14	$49.96	$46.16	$44.37	$43.47
$5,000	$73.92	$62.45	$57.70	$55.46	$54.34
$6,000	$88.71	$74.94	$69.23	$66.55	$65.21
$7,000	$103.49	$87.42	$80.77	$77.64	$76.07
$8,000	$118.28	$99.91	$92.31	$88.73	$86.94
$9,000	$133.06	$112.40	$103.85	$99.82	$97.81
$10,000	$147.84	$124.89	$115.39	$110.91	$108.67
$15,000	$221.76	$187.33	$173.08	$166.36	$163.01
$20,000	$295.68	$249.77	$230.77	$221.82	$217.34
$25,000	$369.60	$312.21	$288.46	$277.27	$271.68
$30,000	$443.52	$374.66	$346.15	$332.72	$326.01

With an interest rate of 12.75%, your monthly payment will be:

Loan Amount	Number of Years in Term				
	10	15	20	25	30
$35,000	$517.44	$437.10	$403.84	$388.17	$380.35
$40,000	$591.36	$499.54	$461.53	$443.63	$434.68
$45,000	$665.28	$561.98	$519.22	$499.08	$489.02
$50,000	$739.20	$624.42	$576.91	$554.53	$543.35
$55,000	$813.12	$686.87	$634.60	$609.98	$597.69
$60,000	$887.04	$749.31	$692.29	$665.44	$652.02
$65,000	$960.96	$811.75	$749.98	$720.89	$706.36
$70,000	$1,034.88	$874.19	$807.67	$776.34	$760.69
$75,000	$1,108.80	$936.63	$865.36	$831.79	$815.02
$80,000	$1,182.72	$999.07	$923.05	$887.25	$869.36
$85,000	$1,256.64	$1,061.52	$980.74	$942.70	$923.69
$90,000	$1,330.56	$1,123.96	$1,038.44	$998.15	$978.03
$95,000	$1,404.48	$1,186.40	$1,096.13	$1,053.60	$1,032.36
$100,000	$1,478.40	$1,248.84	$1,153.82	$1,109.06	$1,086.70
$110,000	$1,626.24	$1,373.73	$1,269.20	$1,219.96	$1,195.37
$120,000	$1,774.08	$1,498.61	$1,384.58	$1,330.87	$1,304.04
$125,000	$1,848.00	$1,561.05	$1,442.27	$1,386.32	$1,358.37
$130,000	$1,921.92	$1,623.49	$1,499.96	$1,441.77	$1,412.71
$140,000	$2,069.76	$1,748.38	$1,615.34	$1,552.68	$1,521.38
$150,000	$2,217.60	$1,873.26	$1,730.72	$1,663.58	$1,630.04
$160,000	$2,365.44	$1,998.14	$1,846.10	$1,774.49	$1,738.71
$170,000	$2,513.28	$2,123.03	$1,961.48	$1,885.39	$1,847.38
$175,000	$2,587.20	$2,185.47	$2,019.18	$1,940.85	$1,901.72
$180,000	$2,661.12	$2,247.91	$2,076.87	$1,996.30	$1,956.05
$190,000	$2,808.96	$2,372.80	$2,192.25	$2,107.20	$2,064.72
$200,000	$2,956.80	$2,497.68	$2,307.63	$2,218.11	$2,173.39
$210,000	$3,104.64	$2,622.56	$2,423.01	$2,329.01	$2,282.06
$220,000	$3,252.48	$2,747.45	$2,538.39	$2,439.92	$2,390.73
$225,000	$3,326.40	$2,809.89	$2,596.08	$2,495.37	$2,445.06
$230,000	$3,400.32	$2,872.33	$2,653.77	$2,550.83	$2,499.40
$240,000	$3,548.16	$2,997.21	$2,769.15	$2,661.73	$2,608.07
$250,000	$3,696.00	$3,122.10	$2,884.53	$2,772.64	$2,716.74
$260,000	$3,843.84	$3,246.98	$2,999.92	$2,883.54	$2,825.41
$270,000	$3,991.68	$3,371.86	$3,115.30	$2,994.45	$2,934.08
$275,000	$4,065.60	$3,434.31	$3,172.99	$3,049.90	$2,988.41
$280,000	$4,139.52	$3,496.75	$3,230.68	$3,105.35	$3,042.75
$290,000	$4,287.36	$3,621.63	$3,346.06	$3,216.26	$3,151.42
$300,000	$4,435.20	$3,746.52	$3,461.44	$3,327.16	$3,260.08
$310,000	$4,583.04	$3,871.40	$3,576.82	$3,438.07	$3,368.75
$320,000	$4,730.88	$3,996.28	$3,692.20	$3,548.97	$3,477.42
$325,000	$4,804.80	$4,058.73	$3,749.89	$3,604.42	$3,531.76
$330,000	$4,878.72	$4,121.17	$3,807.58	$3,659.88	$3,586.09
$340,000	$5,026.56	$4,246.05	$3,922.96	$3,770.78	$3,694.76
$350,000	$5,174.40	$4,370.93	$4,038.35	$3,881.69	$3,803.43
$360,000	$5,322.24	$4,495.82	$4,153.73	$3,992.59	$3,912.10
$370,000	$5,470.08	$4,620.70	$4,269.11	$4,103.50	$4,020.77
$375,000	$5,544.00	$4,683.14	$4,326.80	$4,158.95	$4,075.10
$380,000	$5,617.92	$4,745.59	$4,384.49	$4,214.40	$4,129.44
$390,000	$5,765.76	$4,870.47	$4,499.87	$4,325.31	$4,238.11
$400,000	$5,913.60	$4,995.35	$4,615.25	$4,436.21	$4,346.78

Appendix B

Finding Your Loan Balance

The table shows the percent of the original loan balance that remains outstanding on a standard fixed-rate mortgage with equal monthly payments. The payments on such a mortgage are "fully amortizing," which means that the balance will be extinguished with the final payment. That is the 360th payment on a 30-year loan, the 180th payment on a 15-year loan.

Find the interest rate and original term of your mortgage, and the number of years you are currently into the mortgage. Multiply the decimal listed times the original loan amount to find the balance after the number of years specified.

For example, if you took out a 30-year loan at 6% and the loan is now 5 years old, the decimal is .9305436. If the original loan amount was $100,000, the balance after 5 years is $100,000 times .9305436, or $93,054.

If you don't find your interest rate, you will have to interpolate. Suppose your rate was 5.875%, for example. Since this is midway between 5.75% and 6%, find the cell decimals of both and average them. The cell decimal of 6% after 5 years is .9305436, that of 5.75% is .9276219, and the average is .92908. If the loan was for $100,000, the balance would be approximately $92,908.

The tables will not work if you have made extra payments to principal, have an interest-only option on your mortgage that you have exercised, or if it is an adjustable rate. These situations can be handled using spreadsheets that can be downloaded from my Web site.

Interest Rate	Percent Remaining in Year		
	11	12	13
4.00%	0.5488471	0.4971422	0.4433308
4.25%	0.5549244	0.5032007	0.4492355
4.50%	0.5609791	0.5092469	0.4551382
4.75%	0.5670095	0.5152790	0.4610372
5.00%	0.5730139	0.5212953	0.4669308
5.25%	0.5789907	0.5272942	0.4728174
5.50%	0.5849383	0.5332740	0.4786954
5.75%	0.5908553	0.5392330	0.4845631
6.00%	0.5967400	0.5451698	0.4904189
6.25%	0.6025910	0.5510826	0.4962612
6.50%	0.6084069	0.5569701	0.5020885
6.75%	0.6141863	0.5628307	0.5078993
7.00%	0.6199279	0.5686629	0.5136920
7.25%	0.6256303	0.5744654	0.5194653
7.50%	0.6312924	0.5802367	0.5252176
7.75%	0.6369128	0.5859756	0.5309475
8.00%	0.6424905	0.5916807	0.5366538
8.25%	0.6480243	0.5973508	0.5423350
8.50%	0.6535132	0.6029846	0.5479898
8.75%	0.6589561	0.6085810	0.5536170
9.00%	0.6643521	0.6141389	0.5592154
9.25%	0.6697002	0.6196571	0.5647837
9.50%	0.6749995	0.6251346	0.5703207
9.75%	0.6802493	0.6305704	0.5758255
10.00%	0.6854486	0.6359636	0.5812969
10.25%	0.6905969	0.6413132	0.5867338
10.50%	0.6956934	0.6466184	0.5921352
10.75%	0.7007374	0.6518783	0.5975003
11.00%	0.7057283	0.6570922	0.6028280
11.25%	0.7106656	0.6622593	0.6081175
11.50%	0.7155488	0.6673789	0.6133679
11.75%	0.7203774	0.6724503	0.6185784
12.00%	0.7251510	0.6774730	0.6237483

Interest Rate	Percent Remaining in Year		
	14	15	16
4.00%	0.3873271	0.3290417	0.2683816
4.25%	0.3929315	0.3341874	0.2728975
4.50%	0.3985437	0.3393492	0.2774354
4.75%	0.4041620	0.3445256	0.2819940
5.00%	0.4097848	0.3497152	0.2865723
5.25%	0.4154108	0.3549166	0.2911690
5.50%	0.4210381	0.3601285	0.2957831
5.75%	0.4266654	0.3653494	0.3004134
6.00%	0.4322910	0.3705780	0.3050586
6.25%	0.4379135	0.3758128	0.3097177
6.50%	0.4435314	0.3810526	0.3143895
6.75%	0.4491431	0.3862959	0.3190727
7.00%	0.4547473	0.3915414	0.3237664
7.25%	0.4603424	0.3967878	0.3284693
7.50%	0.4659271	0.4020338	0.3331802
7.75%	0.4715000	0.4072780	0.3378981
8.00%	0.4770596	0.4125191	0.3426219
8.25%	0.4826047	0.4177560	0.3473503
8.50%	0.4881339	0.4229873	0.3520823
8.75%	0.4936460	0.4282118	0.3568169
9.00%	0.4991396	0.4334283	0.3615529
9.25%	0.5046136	0.4386357	0.3662893
9.50%	0.5100667	0.4438327	0.3710250
9.75%	0.5154979	0.4490181	0.3757590
10.00%	0.5209058	0.4541910	0.3804903
10.25%	0.5262895	0.4593501	0.3852178
10.50%	0.5316478	0.4644945	0.3899407
10.75%	0.5369798	0.4696231	0.3946578
11.00%	0.5422844	0.4747348	0.3993684
11.25%	0.5475606	0.4798286	0.4040713
11.50%	0.5528075	0.4849037	0.4087659
11.75%	0.5580242	0.4899590	0.4134510
12.00%	0.5632099	0.4949937	0.4181260

Interest Rate	Percent Remaining in Year		
	17	18	19
4.00%	0.2052502	0.1395467	0.0711663
4.25%	0.2089515	0.1422341	0.0726254
4.50%	0.2126772	0.1449441	0.0740994
4.75%	0.2164267	0.1476761	0.0755879
5.00%	0.2201989	0.1504296	0.0770909
5.25%	0.2239930	0.1532041	0.0786080
5.50%	0.2278082	0.1559989	0.0801390
5.75%	0.2316435	0.1588135	0.0816836
6.00%	0.2354982	0.1616474	0.0832416
6.25%	0.2393712	0.1644999	0.0848128
6.50%	0.2432618	0.1673706	0.0863968
6.75%	0.2471690	0.1702587	0.0879933
7.00%	0.2510919	0.1731638	0.0896022
7.25%	0.2550297	0.1760852	0.0912232
7.50%	0.2589814	0.1790223	0.0928558
7.75%	0.2629462	0.1819746	0.0945000
8.00%	0.2669231	0.1849414	0.0961553
8.25%	0.2709114	0.1879222	0.0978216
8.50%	0.2749100	0.1909164	0.0994984
8.75%	0.2789182	0.1939233	0.1011856
9.00%	0.2829351	0.1969423	0.1028829
9.25%	0.2869597	0.1999730	0.1045899
9.50%	0.2909914	0.2030146	0.1063063
9.75%	0.2950291	0.2060666	0.1080320
10.00%	0.2990721	0.2091284	0.1097665
10.25%	0.3031196	0.2121995	0.1115096
10.50%	0.3071707	0.2152792	0.1132610
10.75%	0.3112247	0.2183671	0.1150204
11.00%	0.3152806	0.2214624	0.1167876
11.25%	0.3193379	0.2245647	0.1185623
11.50%	0.3233956	0.2276735	0.1203441
11.75%	0.3274531	0.2307881	0.1221328
12.00%	0.3315096	0.2339080	0.1239281

Notes

Notes

Notes

Notes

AGY-5407

Notes